Samuel H. Chester

Lights and Shadows of Mission Work in the Far East

Being the Record of Observations Made During a Visit to the Southern Presbyterian Missions

in Japan, China, and Korea in the year 1897

Samuel H. Chester

Lights and Shadows of Mission Work in the Far East
Being the Record of Observations Made During a Visit to the Southern Presbyterian Missions in Japan, China, and Korea in the year 1897

ISBN/EAN: 9783743395299

Manufactured in Europe, USA, Canada, Australia, Japa

Cover: Foto ©ninafisch / pixelio.de

Manufactured and distributed by brebook publishing software (www.brebook.com)

Samuel H. Chester

Lights and Shadows of Mission Work in the Far East

LIGHTS AND SHADOWS

OF

MISSION WORK

IN

THE FAR EAST:

BEING THE RECORD OF OBSERVATIONS MADE DURING A
VISIT TO THE SOUTHERN PRESBYTERIAN MISSIONS
IN JAPAN, CHINA AND KOREA IN THE YEAR 1897.

BY

S. H. CHESTER, D. D.,

SECRETARY OF FOREIGN MISSIONS IN THE PRESBYTERIAN CHURCH
IN THE UNITED STATES.

RICHMOND, VA.:
THE PRESBYTERIAN COMMITTEE OF PUBLICATION.

Copyright

BY

JAMES K. HAZEN, *Secretary of Publication*,

1899.

PRINTED BY
WHITTET & SHEPPERSON,
RICHMOND, VA.

TO MY FRIEND,

WILLIAM HENRY GRANT,

WHOSE GENEROUS KINDNESS MADE THE EXPERIENCES

HEREIN RECORDED POSSIBLE;

AND TO THE

MISSIONARIES IN CHINA, JAPAN AND KOREA,

WHOSE WARMTH OF WELCOME

MADE THEM ALTOGETHER DELIGHTFUL.

PREFACE.

In the autumn of 1897 the author made a visit to the missions of the Southern Presbyterian Church in Japan, China and Korea. The visit was too hurried to admit of very extensive taking of notes, and the plan was adopted of jotting down mnemonics that would serve to recall such things as, on a first view of them, specially interested him, and were in some way connected with the missionary problem and missionary life. An account of these observations has been given in a series of addresses made in a few of our churches and church courts. The renewed interest in missions that has seemed to be awakened by these addresses where they were delivered, and the impossibility of reaching more than a small section of the church in that way, has led to the preparation of this little volume, which, it is hoped, may find its way into missionary libraries and homes in all parts of the church.

Of the books which the author's happy exemption from sea-sickness enabled him to read during the voyage, and found helpful in enabling him to have a better understanding of some things which he saw, he would make special mention of "Problems of the Far East" by Hon. George N. Curzon, which, while none too sympathetic in its references to the missionary work, is exceedingly happy in its descriptive chapters, and most thoughtful and just in its reflections on the social and political conditions of the countries treated of. For a fuller and more adequate description of a Chinese city, especially, than that given in the text the reader is referred to the description of Peking in Mr. Curzon's book, pp. 229-259.

This book is given its local coloring from the fact that the author's visit was especially to the Southern Presbyterian Missions. But, as mission work and mission problems are of largely the same character with all Protestant missions, it is believed that the matter the book contains will be found of general interest. If any dull hearts are stirred by it to more prayer and helpfulness in the mission work in his own or other churches, the author will be more than satisfied and amply repaid for his labors.

NASHVILLE, TENN.

CONTENTS.

CHAPTER I.
To the Far East, ... 9

CHAPTER II.
The Country and People of Japan, . . 15

CHAPTER III.
New Japan and Christian Missions, . . 28

CHAPTER IV.
The Country and People of China, . . 46

CHAPTER V.
The Missionary Problem and Work in China, 65

CHAPTER VI.
Hindrances and Results, ... 77

CHAPTER VII.
The Country and People of Korea, . . 91

CHAPTER VIII.
Mission Work in Korea, ... 114

Mission Work in the Far East.

CHAPTER I.

To the Far East.

Those of my readers who may be meditating the possibility of a foreign tour will do well, before determining the direction of their travels, at least to consider the relative claims of Europe and Asia. The one advantage on the side of Europe, it seems to me, is the shortness of the time required for the journey. For the same length of time the expense of the Asiatic tour is far less. The things seen are more interesting because so utterly unlike what one has ever seen before. The flavor of immemorial antiquity and of associations connected with the infancy of our race lend an added charm. And one interested in the triumph of God's kingdom on earth will find in the Far East especially the place where the battle is now on which is to determine whether the gospel is stronger than the powers of evil intrenched in their most ancient strongholds.

Looking at the matter from a more worldly and prosaic standpoint, it is doubtful whether, for purposes of absolute rest, human experience furnishes anything quite equal to a voyage across the Pacific in the month of August. Our good ship is indeed a "lodge in a vast wilderness" of waters, where no rumor of business cares can reach us; the sea is even monotonously placid, and we grow just weary enough of the "boundless contiguity" of sea and sky to experience the full effect of the vision of green hills and purple waters when the island of Oahu first greets us through the morning mist. On this island is the city of Honolulu, the metropolis and seat of government of the Hawaiian group. Although it is within the tropics, the climate at Honolulu is so modified by a cold current from our northwestern coast that the maximum temperature in summer is only 87° Fahrenheit. The minimum in winter is 55°. Whether viewed from the outside, or entered and explored, it presents us everywhere with views of enchanting loveliness. Looking down from the top of the Punch Bowl or the Pali, one might imagine himself, as Bayard Taylor says, "standing on the Delectable

The voyage.

Our new possessions.

HAWAIIAN FISHERMAN.

Mountains, with the valleys of the land of Beulah spread out before him." Standing in the valley and looking at the mountains shrouded in mist, and the gorges arched over with rainbows, the suggestion is of Bunyan's dream of the gates and towers of the Celestial City. Royal palms, cocoanut trees, spreading banyans, oleanders, the pomegranate, the orange, mimosas, banana groves, all manner of trailing vines, with flowers of every hue, are everywhere. All this flora has been imported, the soil of volcanic origin being originally devoid of such vegetation. But, once planted, it flourishes in the richest tropical luxuriance.

The physiognomy of the native strongly suggests the East Indian origin which tradition also ascribes to him. He has a fairly well-shaped head well set on broad, square shoulders, a large and muscular-looking physique, and an attractive face. But he is lacking in toughness of fibre, his eyes are dull and his brain is pulpy. The women especially show an early inclination to obesity, for which they are only the more admired. The first civilized dress introduced among them was the "Mother Hubbard" wrapper, and to it they still almost universally adhere. One good of it, considering the sudorific qualities of the climate, is that is does not adhere much to them. In spite of their wealth of black hair and the beautiful flower wreaths worn on their hats, they do not achieve much in the way of picturesque appearance, except when riding a bicycle or on horseback astride.

I expected to see an exhibition of barbaric splendor in the Government House where the representative of our government now sits in the chair of the ousted Queen. But it is simply a neat stucco building, with tasteful interior finishings, but nothing loud or gaudy about it. In the Bishop Museum one may still see the gorgeous feather cloaks once worn by the Kamehamehas on occasions of state, the large circular wooden "calabashes," or trays, dug out and polished to a wonderful smoothness by stone implements, and the ropes, some with stains of blood still on them, once used in strangling human sacrifices, and the large hooks once used to fish for sharks, with a piece of a Hawaiian for bait. But these now possess even for the native only an antiquarian interest.

The Americans who have found a home in this "Paradise of the Pacific," about three thousand in number, have first civilized it, then appropriated it, and then generously donated it to their home government. Without raising the question of abstract right

American enterprise.

involved in these proceedings, it may be said that whatever was done that, from a theoretical standpoint, might seem high-handed, has the justification of having been done for the sake of self-preservation; and it cannot be denied that the whole result has been beneficial to the natives. The introduction by the early navigators of civilized vices, diseases, rum and gunpowder reduced their numbers during the century from 400,000 to about 40,000. But under the influence of the schools, colleges and churches with which the islands are now covered, and of the orderly administration of government given them by the Americans, their numbers are now increasing again, and their condition is in every way unspeakably better that it ever was under their native rulers. What further will become of this interesting people as the wards of our nation remains for time to disclose. Let it be hoped that the public sentiment of the twentieth century will tolerate nothing but justice and kindness in our dealings with them. Our brief glimpse of them and their lovely island home was only an episode of our journey to the Far East. Ten days more of quiet and restful sailing, with only an occasional grateful gale, just strong enough to clear the ship of the odors rising from the Chinese steerage, brings us in sight of land again. Presently our ship casts anchor in Yokohama Bay, and we hasten ashore to see the things new and old which the wonderful Sunrise Kingdom has to show us for our instruction and delight.

CHAPTER II.

The Country and People of Japan.

Physical features. Many exaggerated ideas are abroad in regard to Japan, but one thing concerning which we can scarcely have an exaggerated idea is the physical beauty of the country. In sailing around the world one will pass in view of many goodly islands and charming landscapes, but of none that surpass in beauty those that greet us in our passage through the Inland Sea. The vision of them, left behind, lingers with the traveller ever afterwards like memory of a lovely dream. And where, among mountains, shall we find the peer of Fuji, visible far out at sea, standing up like a sentinel to guard the coast, twelve thousand feet high, an almost perfect cone, and crowned with perpetual snow?

Of the total area of the country about two-thirds is occupied by mountains, not brown and bare like most of those we see in China and Korea, but covered with green foliage, or terraced and cultivated to the very top. Long avenues lined with the lofty and graceful cryptomoria lead back to picturesque little shrines, or to great and gorgeous temples, in dark shaded groves. The cherry blossoms in the spring, the azaleas in summer, the maple leaves in autumn, or the ice crystals on evergreen trees in winter, light up the glens and gorges with a perennial blaze of glory. No wonder the people love their beautiful islands with a devotion so intense that some esteem it to be even foolish, and call them "the land of the gods."

But there is an element of terror also mingled with the beauty in the aspect of nature in Japan. Among these lovely mountains there are hundreds of extinct volcanoes and about twenty that are still alive. The tradition of Fuji is that it was heaved up from the ocean in a single night about three thousand years ago, and its history is that one night, about three hundred years ago, the whole top of it blew off with a great explosion, scattering broken rocks and lava far and wide and covering the streets of Tokio, sixty miles away, with ashes. In the autumn that most extensive and violent form of the cyclone, known as the "typhoon," sweeps across both land and water, leaving wreck and ruin in its track. . There is an average of one earthquake a day, some of them mere tremors, but others so violent as to reduce whole villages to ruins. Accom-

MISSION WORK IN THE FAR EAST. 17

panying the earthquakes huge tidal waves sometimes sweep over the coasts, in one of which, a few years ago, more than 30,000 lives were destroyed. The rivers which up in the mountains are little rivulets, playing and cascading over beautiful white rocks, are filled in the spring by the melting snows with floods that go raging down into the plains, sweeping away dikes and bridges and covering thousands of acres of prosperous farms with silt and gravel.

<small>Characteristics.</small> The character of the people is plainly marked by both of these features of their government, being a combination of tragic moodiness with a sort of playful æstheticism.

The æsthetic faculty is strong in all classes. The wealthy spare no pains or expense on their gardens of ornamental shrubbery and flowers. In the back yard of every house, important enough to have a back yard, flowers of many kinds, and especially the royal chrysanthemum, are cultivated in their highest perfection. The school boy's table is adorned with flowers, and the farmer returning from his day's work in the field will stop by the way to admire the beauty of a budding peach tree. In the spring when the cherries are in bloom they go out in great pic-nicking crowds to see and enjoy them.

On the other hand, in the summer, bands of pilgrims, dressed in their white mourning costumes, go to the top of Fuji to worship there the gods of the storm and earthquake. Suicide is their refuge from trouble, about 7,000 a year being regarded as a conservative estimate of the number. The favorite method in the older time among the soldier class was that known as *"hari-kari"* (belly-cutting.) Before the weapons of modern warfare were introduced every soldier wore two swords, a long one for his enemies and a short one for himself. When defeat or calamity overtook him he would sit on the floor of his hall with his friends around him and insert the short sword into his side and draw it across the abdomen, after which a friend would complete the operation of *hari-kari* by cutting off his head. This was indeed a "shuffling off" of the mortal coil, and reveals a strong element of the tragic in those who would choose that method of making their exit from the world.

The Japanese present a commendable contrast with other Orientals in the matter of personal cleanliness. Rumor says that, about the first of October, the average Chinaman takes his farewell bath until the return of warm weather the following spring. But he is regarded as unworthy of the name of a Japanese, whether he

be nobleman or peasant, who does not bathe once
a day in water just below the boiling point. The
unpainted woodwork of their houses is all thoroughly scrubbed once a year. Their floors are
covered with beautiful white straw matting,
always kept immaculately clean. To this end,
on entering a house, all shoes must be left at the
front door. This does not greatly incommode
the native whose shoe is a wooden or straw san-
dal that can be readily shuffled off or on, but it
tends to make life a burden to the foreigner with
laced gaiters, and also to the development of endless colds and catarrhs and influenzas. The
only heating apparatus is the *Hibachi,* a small
jar filled with pulverized ashes with a few
lumps of live charcoal on top, by which one can
warm his hands after a fashion, but which gives
off more carbonic gas than heat to the atmosphere of the room. Natives and missionaries
keep their feet warm by sitting on the soles of
them turned up behind. The transient traveller whose joints have not been educated to this
posture must make the best he can of cold feet,
unless he is able to effect a compromise with custom, as I did, by means of a pair of crocheted
over-slippers furnished me by one of the ladies
of our mission. By the discreet use of these
both the traveller's health and reputation for

politeness may in some measure be saved. Since the days of Abraham and Ephron the Hittite, at least, we know that dignity and politeness of demeanor have been characteristic of Orientals. But in these qualities also the Japanese stand pre-eminent. When a visitor enters a room they bow, usually three times, until the body and legs are at right angles. If sitting, they lean over three times until the forehead almost touches the floor. The use of multiplied honorifics and self-depreciations, and the constant iteration of deferential grunts and inhalations is a serious hindrance to rational conversation. This politeness is characteristic of all classes, and any common coolie among them would lay the courteousness of our "old time gentleman" entirely in the shade. They are the Frenchmen of the East, and, like the Frenchmen of the West, very much of their overdone politeness is only surface deep. But on the whole they are to be commended for it, and one feels the contrast painfully on coming immediately from Japan to America and coming in contact with the railroad manners of our great west.

The people are almost dwarfishly small of stature, but have great power of physical endurance. I tested some of them—as well as myself—thoroughly in that respect on an overland journey from Kochi to Tokushima, a distance of 110 miles, which, in company with Rev. J. W. Moore and Rev. S. R. Hope, of the Southern Presbyterian Mission, I covered in two days. Our vehicle was the famous *jin-rick-sha,* a comfortable little sulky pulled by a man instead of a horse. The name means literally "Pull-man-car." The way was over one of the old military roads found throughout the Empire, some of them said to date from the second century of our era, and was graded for more than half the way through a mountain pass. It was about eighteen feet wide, the mountains rising sheer up on one side and a mountain torrent foaming over the rocks at the bottom of a precipice about one hundred feet deep on the other. An incidental discovery of the journey was that one of the many things the Japanese have no fear of is a precipice. Houses were built all along the edge of this one, with no barriers to keep the children from falling over, and no one manifesting any anxiety lest they should fall. Small children with other small children on their backs were frequently seen standing on its edge and peering over into its depths. In going around holes and ruts, in spite of our protestations, our men *would* go every time on the side of the precipice instead of on the side of the mountain.

They continued this perverse line of conduct in the same *non-chalant* and half-amused way even after Mr. Moore's vehicle had actually capsized and pitched him over the precipice, fortunately, however, at place where there was a ledge a short distance below the road that caught him. We travelled forty-five miles the first day with no change of men and sixty-five miles the second day with three changes. The *rick-sha* man in costume looks much like a college athlete equipped for the running match, is very proud of his muscle and speed, and always assumes a rapid and high-stepping gait when passing through a village. A good one will easily cover a distance of fifty miles on a good road in ten hours. What the Japanese lack in size they also make up in spirit and courage. The Chinese contemptuously call them *"wojen"*—island dwarfs. But as the Chinese have more than once found, to their sorrow, they have ever been a most unsatisfactory people for enemies to encounter in war. Zinghis-Khan, with his Tartars, overran China, and his grandson, Kublai-Khan, thought to do the same thing with Japan, supposing, no doubt, that he would have quite a holiday time with the little islanders. The expedition, fitted out with much pomp and circumstance, reached the shores of Japan, but never landed. It would have re-

FEUDAL CASTLE AT NAGOYA

turned much wiser than it came except that only three men of it survived to tell the tale. The war-like propensities of the Japanese seem to have been among their original and permanent traits and not a recent development. Each provincial city has its ancient castle, the stronghold of the old *Daimio,* who held fief of the Mikado to rule the province. A fine specimen of these is the one at Nagoya. It is built of huge blocks of stone, its two main towers being 170 feet high and crowned with figures representing dolphins of enormous size and covered with beaten gold. It is surrounded by a moat that can be filled with water or emptied at pleasure. Its base is large enough to furnish storage room for several months supply of provisions, so that the old feudal lord, even though he might not be strong enough to come out and fight in the open, could look out from his observation tower and smile at all his foes. In the old days of fighting with swords the sword of the Samura had the temper of a razor, and the enemy who came within its sweep was almost sure to emerge from the encounter minus a head. From the earliest days of their recorded history to this day the soil of Japan has never been successfully invaded by a foreign enemy. They have now an army of about 250,000 men, including reserves, drilled and equipped after the latest models, and, except in the cavalry wing of it, hardly less formidable, man for man, than that of any western power. They have a navy that is second in fighting power only to that of England in the waters of the Far East. And in the light of present day developments one wonders sometimes if we may not some day see them united with England and America in an invincible alliance for human freedom, not only in the Orient, but in the world.

The old national religion of Japan is Shintoism—"the way of the gods." It is a strange religion with a strange name, inasmuch as it takes no account of any gods, nor of morality in any form. Its moral postulate is that obedience to the Emperor is the whole duty of man, and that, as for the rest, all a Japanese needs to be perfect is to follow the bent of his nature, which will always lead him right. In later times it entered into a fusion with Confucianism, with which it had some things in common, the resultant combination being a sort of *apotheosis* of patriotism, loyalty and obedience to "the powers that be." This is to a large extent the religion, or substitute for religion, of the upper and educated classes.

Buddhism prevails among the masses, and is

BUDDHA, NARA, JAPAN.

Height, 53 feet; face, 16 x 9 feet; eye-brows, 5 feet; mouth, 3½ feet. Five hundred pounds of gold, 16,000 pounds of tin, over 20,000 pounds of copper, besides iron, used in casting. Date, 1150 A. D.

more alive in Japan than it is even in India, the land of its birth. Nowhere else are the temples so numerous, so costly, so well kept, or so thronged with worshippers. Their gold candelabra, their bronze filigree, their lacquered chests, their fretted ceilings of blue and gilt and red wrought in lotus flowers, butterflies and various mythical figures, all as fresh and clean as the day they were made, present a contrast indeed to the dingy old temples of China. The vitality of Buddhism, though probably somewhat diminished of late years, is still everywhere in evidence.

As to the general moral result there is much difference of opinion. Sir Edwin Arnold and Mr. Lafcadio Hearn are delighted with it. The national custom of promiscuous bathing and the general indifference of both sexes to the exposure of their persons is pointed to by some of their romantic admirers as a sign of their Edenic innocence. But the impartial observer may find himself forced to see in such things both a sign and a cause of the opposite condition. The census of 1895 reported an average of one divorce to every three marriages, and in every city the signs of legalized social immorality are most painfully abundant. In the foreign banks and business houses in the coast cities it has been found necessary to employ Chinese instead of Japanese in positions of trust. Japanese trade will have a more permanent prosperity when their silk, which they sell by weight, is found on inspection to have less chalk in it, when a larger proportion of their matches will strike, and when the repudiation of contracts discovered to be unprofitable becomes less common. Judged even by Oriental and heathen standards, it seems to me that the Japanese must be pronounced to be rather below than above *par* in the matter of every-day morals. On the other hand, their riddance of the curse of a professional official class, like the Mandarins of China and the Yangbans of Korea, their national pride and desire to appear well in the eyes of civilized nations, and the subjection of rulers to the criticism of an active and out-spoken public press have lifted them far above all other eastern nations in their political morality. At present, by the operation of the revised treaties, they are just coming into the fraternity of civilized nations on terms of recognized equality. It will mean much for the welfare of other countries in the Far East as well as for herself if Japan shall so deport herself in this new *role* as to justify the action of the powers in yielding her this recognition. The missionary body, who constitute much the largest portion of her foreign residents, will rejoice, for her sake as well as for their own, if she succeeds in doing so. It is they also who have done most in the past to make such recognition possible, and who will do most in the future to make her worthy of it. And it is a hopeful sign that this is now being acknowledged by some of her leading statesmen.

CHAPTER III.

New Japan and Christian Missions.

The Japanese are intellectually bright and quick, with a consuming thirst for knowledge, especially of things that are supposed to be new. They have never been characterized by the false pride and conservatism that have well nigh petrified and mummified China, but have always been ready to examine new ideas, and to welcome them if they seemed better than what they had, from whatever source they might come. They readily exchanged their old barbarism for the civilization of China when it was brought to them, and no more hesitate to acknowledge their obligations to Confucius than if he had been a native Japanese. So, when our western civilization was brought to them they had an open eye for its advantages, and, after a little preliminary dallying, made such a rush for it as has no parallel in the history of civilization. In thirty years time they have set up and put in full operation a system of parliamentary government under a written constitution. The Emperor, though still nominally absolute, rules practically through his cabinet and parliament, like the constitutional sovereigns of Europe. Under the feudal system the old *Daimios* not only had the power of life and death themselves, but their retainers (the *Samurai*) were privileged to swish off the heads of the common people with their razor-like swords on the slightest provocation. These have now been required to step down and out, leaving justice to be administered by courts of law, under written codes framed on European models. A school system has been organized that ascends in regular gradation from the primary school with compulsory attendance through the middle school, high school and college, and culminates in the great Imperial University at Tokyo, which receives an annual appropriation from the government of about $200,000. They have better postal and telegraph facilities than we have, and countless numbers of daily, weekly and monthly publications, the city of Tokyo alone having seventeen daily papers. The streets of the larger cities are fast being equipped with electric cars and lights. Nearly two thousand miles of railway are in operation, the great commercial centres from Tokyo to Kobe being connected by a line over which two through trains a day are run without change. So far as the external features of our civilization therefore are concerned, Japan has them in abundance.

What then lacks she yet? Much every way, and especially she lacks yet the infiltration of true civilization into the character of her people; and she lacks the spirit of it *which is Christianity.*

In the streets of Nagasaki I met a native gentleman dressed in a Derby hat, a steam laundered shirt and collar, a silk cravat, and over these a linen duster. The upper half of him was thus Christianly arrayed, but the lower half of him was not arrayed at all. He was a walking allegory. Japan is civilized at the top, but not at the bottom. Out in the country among the common people one sees many more relics of primitive savagery than among the Chinese, or even the Koreans. She is also civilized on the outside, but not yet on the inside to any great degree. And whether this external civilization of ours will in the long run do her more good than evil, depends on whether we shall succeed in our effort to give her along with it our Christian religion, which alone can effect that regeneration of character which can make Japan or any other nation truly civilized and great.

<small>Christian missions.</small> Among the other Western things that Japan rushed at for a time was Christianity. When the feudal system was overthrown the feudal retainers, who were soldiers,

scholars, and gentry all in one, found themselves in the new order of things without a reason of existence. Some of them went abroad and studied in foreign schools. Of these some became real Christians, and others, finding a convenient mode of subsistence in lecturing in churches and practicing on the credulity of the Christian public, became Christians for the sake of the loaves and fishes. On their return they naturally became associated with the missionaries from the countries they had visited, and found at once a sphere of usefulness and a means of livelihood as the missionaries' teachers, interpreters, and helpers. They reported also to the men of their class that the civilization they so much admired was allied in the West with Christianity. Christianity thus gradually became popular with the Samurai. Meanwhile many of them had also turned politicians, and come to occupy positions of influence in the government; and as churches grew and multiplied they were found to have a goodly number of lawyers, judges, and members of parliament on their rolls, and there was even some foolish talk of having Christianity adopted as the national religion. The churches and missionary boards were very naturally, but, as it seems to me, not very wisely or scripturally, elated, and much was made in missionary magazines of the fact that we had obtained a foothold among the "better classes" in Japan, and much was hoped from their influence for the rapid evangelization of the country. In twenty years from the time the first Protestant church was organized in Yokohama about 40,000 converts had been enrolled, the great majority of them being from this Samurai class.

Just at this point a sudden and unexpected turning of the tide set in, and now for some years past our Protestant missions in Japan, instead of marching on to swift and glorious victory, have found themselves hard pressed to hold their own. Some writers express the opinion that this reaction has spent its force, and that we may now expect to see the native church enter on another period of rapid growth. I cannot see that the present situation has any such promise, nor do I think it desirable that we see any more "boom times" in the experience of our Japan missions. The prosperity of the early years was in many respects only seeming, and the present situation is the natural outcome of some things that were an element of that seeming prosperity. I think a partial explanation of the reaction is to be found in the following facts.

A reaction.

First, the available material in the class which had been the special object of evangelistic effort was about exhausted. This class numbered only about 80,000 in the empire, and when 40,000 of them had been enrolled as communing members in the churches we can readily see that there was not much field for further enlargement in that direction. If all of these had been Christians after the type of Joseph Neesima they would have made an evangelistic force that would have been irresistible. But many of them had simply come in on the popular wave, and their motives were everything else but spiritual. Many others, who were real Christians, were unfortified by any thorough instruction in Christian doctrine and characterized by all the native instability and love of that which was new.

Then, "while men slept, the enemy came and sowed tares among the wheat." Never was there a more striking illustration of this devil's strategy, and never was there a more fruitful soil for tares to grow in than in the minds of these nimble-witted, novelty-loving, vivacious, and volatile Japanese. Rationalists from this country and from Europe went over and made them believe that *they* represented the new, the advanced, the improved phases of Christian thought in the west, while the earlier missionaries, with their infallible Bible and their formulated creeds, represented only what was old and effete. The reason that these heresies, instead of merely weakening the church's spiritual power and checking its growth, did not work utter havoc and devastation with it, is because there was an element in it which had learned, in a genuine experience, and in the fires of persecution, the divine power of God's inspired word and the preciousness of Christ's atoning blood. But this element was not strong enough to overcome all the reactionary tendencies, and did not itself wholly escape being affected by them.

It was found also that the class spirit, which is a trouble everywhere, but is peculiarly strong in Oriental countries, began to assert itself and to make our church of the "better classes" less zealous than it should have been in carrying the gospel to those below them. To expect that this would be otherwise is more than the history of even regenerate human nature warrants us in expecting of it.

And so the history of our Japan missions, looked at from the standpoint of the hopes once cherished of them, has been somewhat disappointing.

There has been disappointment also in another direction from which much was once ex-

Educational results. pected. The first missionaries who went out found themselves much restricted in the matter of residence and travel, and also in the privilege of openly preaching the gospel. But their services were in demand as teachers, and they took the lead in the new educational movement, hoping that this would at least undermine the old idolatries and prepare the way for the gospel. If this movement had continued under missionary auspices it might have had this result, but meanwhile Japanese young men were going abroad to study in foreign schools. When they returned with their degrees they very naturally wished themselves to fill the places in their native schools, and in course of time, except for the purpose of teaching English, the foreign teachers were largely supplanted by them. Most of them came back mentally saturated with the views of Huxley and Spencer, or whatever they had come in contact with that claimed to be new in western science and philosophy. The whole government educational system is now under their control and has become, not only anti-Christian, but thoroughly materialistic and atheistic.

The following facts will show to what extent this kind of education has undermined the old idolatries. If it has done so with a few of the higher classes, it does not seem, in their case, to have prepared the way for the gospel, but rather for something even worse than what they had before. The famous statesman, Count Ito, may be fairly taken to represent this class. He says, "I regard religion as quite unnecessary to a nation's life. Science is far above superstition, and what is any religion, Buddhism or Christianity, but superstition, and therefore a possible source of weakness to a nation."

Among the masses the old idolatries, instead of disappearing, seem to be taking on new life and vigor, and are seeking now to extend and propagate themselves by methods they have learned from the missionaries. At Kobe, in company with Rev. H. B. Price, I attended a funeral conducted by two priests, one of whom was a woman, at which there was a gorgeous display of flowers and much beating of drums and various spectacular accompaniments. In reply to Mr. Price's inquiry, we were told that the performers represented "a sect of Shinto, somewhat like the Salvation Army." At another place we saw some handsome western style stone buildings which, we were told, were "a Buddhist Theological Seminary," where several hundred young men were being trained for the priesthood.

At Kioto there has just been completed the finest temple ever built in Japan, at a cost of about $2,000,000, which was all met by private contributions, chiefly of the common people. The great wooden pillars of the portico were reared by ropes woven of the hair of many thousands of women, the most precious thing they had to offer, devoted to the purpose. In the enclosure of another great temple we saw some very modern looking machinery at work, which we found was an electric light plant that was being used to furnish light to some carpenters who were repairing the roof of the temple. At Tokio I saw great crowds of people going out on electric cars over a road from which school houses, law courts, parliament houses, steam factories, and all kinds of things belonging to western civilization were in full view to the magnificent and well-kept temples on the outskirts of the city, where they stood, some of them dressed in cut-away coats and Derby hats, and bowed and clapped their hands before the idols of bronze and stone. Some of them chewed wads of paper on which prayers were written and threw them at the idols. If the paper wad stuck, the prayer was supposed to be efficacious; if otherwise, it was offered in vain.

So, as for beautiful and progressive Japan,

the old idolatries are still there; and a much more formidable enemy, *educated atheism,* is also there; and a Christian church is there which is in many respects other than we wish it might be; and this is the missionary problem that now confronts us in that most interesting country.

And now the question is, what is to be done about it?

First of all, it seems to me, some useful lessons lie on the surface of this history that greatly need to be learned, and yet which the church is very slow to learn. Our Master tells us that the missionary anointing he received was, first of all, "to preach the gospel to the poor." If the situation in Palestine in his day had been, as it was in the beginning of our Japan missions, that he had no access to the poor and did have access to the better classes, he would have preached the gospel to them. But we do not think he would have felt any elation at such a state of affairs, nor counted on any special advantage to his cause from their financial, social, political, or other forms of worldly influence. Through the whole course of Christian history whenever the church has leaned upon this broken reed its hand has always, sooner or later, been pierced. In building the church, as in building a house, the best place to begin is at the bottom. As the building progresses the middle and the top will eventually also be reached. Therefore, if in China and Korea or elsewhere our first access is only to the poor and lowly, let us not be discouraged, but rather rejoice on that account, remembering that "God hath chosen the weak things of the world to confound the things which are mighty; that no flesh should glory in his presence."

Again, Japan furnishes a striking object lesson to show that they are mistaken who think that secular education and western material civilization, going in advance of the gospel in any of these old eastern countries, are in any sense a preparation for it. On the contrary, they leave the old barriers unremoved, and erect new and stronger ones in addition to the old for the gospel to overcome. It is too late now to apply this lesson in Japan, but we may apply it in China and Korea. Our experience in Japan should teach the church that this is its day of opportunity in those countries, *to go in and evangelize them first,* so that when our science and civilization reach them, as they speedily will, they will come to Christian instead of to heathen peoples, and do them good instead of harm.

Finally, as to Japan, it may be said that our mission history there has, in a certain sense, followed providential lines; and, although the situation as thus developed be a difficult one to deal with, the very last thing we ought to do is to become discouraged about it. There are some features in it that are full of encouragement and cheer. While the church there at present contains a good deal of chaff and tares, it also contains many earnest, spiritual, and praying men, who, in the battle that is now fully on, will not be found wanting. And while it contains some native preachers who are not as sound and evangelical as they should be, there are also a goodly number who are aware of and mourn over the things that are wrong, and who are ready to be used for the new and different kind of work that is now waiting to be done. I heard one preach on the text, "I am come that they might have life," and the outline of the sermon as given me by Rev. R. E. McAlpine, of our mission, differed from the sermon outline we often see published in our Monday morning papers as a piece of bread differs from a cake of sawdust. The points emphasized were: (1), The high aim of Christ towards men—to give them *life*—as contrasted with Confucius and other teachers. (2), The necessity of this life, men being spiritually dead. (3), The character of it: it is spiritual, penetrating, and saturating the soul, working from within outwards

[marginal note: Encouraging features.]

in the life and character. (4), The spiritual effects of it, illustrated by Christ's miracles of healing; set forth in his sermon on the mount, shown in the lives of his apostles; experienced by us in temptation, poverty, danger, and persecution. (5), If we have this life, shall we selfishly keep the joy of it to ourselves, or try to communicate it to our fellow-men?

Needs.
I think it is inspiring to know that we have native preachers in Japan who can preach sermons like that. The needs of the present time as they impressed themselves on me are, first, a *large increase* of the missionary force. The increase, however, should be only of men able to deal with difficult problems in a wise way, and especially of men whose voices will always ring true on the Bible as an infallible rule of faith, and on the central truths of the old gospel. Then we need a native ministry trained by such missionaries as these, in practical work as well as theology, and taken from the lower classes, so that they will naturally be in sympathy with them. And then we need to go out from the great cities where the few hundreds of thousands live, into all the small towns and villages where the 40,000,000 live, and preach the simple, old, orthodox gospel, until all the people have learned to know and understand what it is. This work

will necessarily be slow and toilsome, largely hand to hand, and unattended by any brilliant and spectacular results. The true kingdom of God will no more come in Japan than it has ever done elsewhere "with observation." But if we will do the will of God in this matter, in faith and patience, then after we have done it we shall inherit the promise. Not by western science and education, nor by political or social influence, nor by any other human influence whatsoever, but only by the foolishness of preaching that gospel which is the wisdom and the power of God, will the old idolatries be finally overthrown, and the idols be cast to the moles and the bats, and Japan become in deed and in truth a Christian nation. On the whole it seemed to me that the conditions that confront our missionaries in Japan are more trying, and their work more difficult, than those of any of the fields I visited. They are standing in their lot bravely, cheerfully, and hopefully, asking of us only our sympathy, our prayers, and our earnest co-operation in their work.

The native Christians also rightly look to us for the same thing. I had a visit from one of the elders of the church at Nagoya, a captain in the army, who came to talk over the situation, and to urge that we should not diminish, but that we should try to enlarge our work among them. He said we had prayed to God to give us churches in Japan, and in answer to our prayers he had given us many, most of which were still in the weakness of infancy. And now to abandon any of these churches and leave them to perish "would not," it seemed to him, "be treating God with proper politeness." So, speaking reverently, as Capt. Hibiti meant his expression, it seemed to me.

What the church needs most of all is the willingness to answer this touching appeal. And the day we ought to look and pray for is the day when it shall be said, *God has made His people willing in the day of His power.*[1]

---

[1] Japan also needs a well endowed Christian school of a grade equal to the best government colleges, the patronage of which would come from the graduates of the mission schools. Only from such a school can we hope to obtain the Christian leaders, both in the ministry and in secular life, that are necessary to the success of the work on any large scale. To guarantee that such a school would remain Christian and orthodox, for the present and for some time to come, both its endowment and its board of management should be retained in this country. If this course had been pursued with the Doshisha, the present unhappy outcome of that enterprise would have been avoided.

The remarks in this chapter concerning unwarranted and unrealized hopes from the effect of Western education and civilization are not intended to imply any depreciation of the right kind of Christian education, which always has been and always will be found to be an essential part of successful missionary work.

Statistics of Christian and Missionary Work in Japan for the Year 1897.

The different Presbyterian bodies working in Japan carry on their work separately as missions, but unitedly as regards "The Church of Christ in Japan," the one body into which the results of all their work are gathered.

NAME OF MISSION.	Year of arrival in Japan.	Missionaries.	Organized churches.	Churches wholly self-supporting.	Churches partially self-supporting.	Baptized adult converts, 1897.	Baptized children.	Total membership.	Sunday-schools.	Scholars in Sunday-schools.	Theological schools.	Theological students.	Native ministers.	Unordained preachers and helpers.	Bible women.	Contributions of native Christians for all purposes.
*Presbyterian Church of the U. S. A.,	1859	49										25			30	
*Reformed Church in America,	1859	30														
*United Presbyterian Church of Scotland,	1874	4									1					
*The Church of Christ in Japan,			70	10	56	774	120	11,108	198	5,415		21	80	125	4	$9,079
*Reformed Church in the United States,	1879	15														
*Presbyterian Church in the U. S. (South),	1885	29										2				
*Woman's Union Missionary Societies, U.S.A.	1871	5						6	260					90	
*Cumberland Presbyterian Church,	1877	14	1		1	3	3	46	4	125	1	3		3	6	
Evangelical Lutheran Mission, U. S. A.,	1892	2	1						49	2,166	1	16	14	49	1	40
American Protestant Episcopal Church,	1859	42													17	
Church Missionary Society,																
Nippon Sei Kokuwai,	1869	81	72	1	71	690	261	8,349	67	1,935	4	22	23	71	18	4,302

Mission	Year															
Society for the Propagation of the Gospel,	1873	14														
St. Andrew's University Mission,		7														
St. Hilda's Mission,		7														
Baptist Missionary Union, America,	1860	54	25	4	21	190		1,870	68	3,251	1	11	6	40	20	895
Baptist Southern Convention,	1889	6	1		1	11		61	3	175	1		1	4	1	50
Disciples of Christ,	1883	15	7		7	45		413	16	900		7	8	5	11	150
Christian Church of America,	1887	5	6		6	45		307	12	740	1	6	4	3	3	160
The Kumi-ai Churches in co-operation with the American Board's Mission,	1869	69	73	38	35	420	747	10,047	135	4,132	2	12	30	63	29	11,462
American Methodist Episcopal Church,	1873	67	55	3	52	518	82	3,524	129	8,055	1	9	56	16	30	8,916
Methodist Church of Canada,	1873	30	22	3	19	116	47	1,807	68	2,640	1	6	2	68	15	2,413
Evangelical Association of North America,	1876	4	14		14	69	21	840	20	589	1	3	17	7	11	560
Methodist Protestant Church,	1880	16	4	1	3	39	8	323	25	916	1	4	4	6		299
Methodist Episcopal Church (South),	1886	34	12	2	10	76	28	559	54	1,554	1	6	3	68	3	1,238
United Brethren in Christ,	1896					38	2	145	3	70			2	10	2	119
Scandinavian Allianco Mission in Japan,	1891	8	1		4	11		116	12	393		1	4	5	2	6
General Evang'l Protestant (German Swiss),	1885	5	1		1	8		106	3	51	1	1	2	1		28
Society of Friends, U. S. A.,	1885	6				18		126	6	220		4		7	1	41
The Christian and Missionary Alliance,	1891	5				7			4	500			1	8		5
Unitarian,	1889	1														
Universalist,	1890	6	3		3	15		76	6	145	1	3	3	6	1	68
Salvation Army,	1895	10	7		7			130	7	511		6	21			168
Hephzibah Faith Missionary Association,	1894	2				3		21	1					2		15
Independent (native),						64		604	5	230		3		7	3	758
Independent (foreign),		10	6	6												
Total of Protestant Missions, 1897,		652	384	72	312	3,062	1,348	40,578	901	35,083	21	169	302	580	299	$40,772

* Church of Christ in Japan.

CHAPTER IV.

The Country and People of China.

The essential difference between Chinese and Japanese native character is shown in the stolid and immovable opposition which China presents to the enlightenment and improvements that have been knocking at her gates for more than half a century from the nations of the West. There is method in China's madness, however, in this matter, for preserving as she has done, almost unchanged, the way of doing things inaugurated by the founder of her nation, who is claimed not without plausible reason to have been the grandson of Noah, the transition to new ways which must come sooner or later will involve a revolution that can hardly be accomplished without a violent disruption of the present social order. Meanwhile, those who would like to see what Oriental life was like at least as far back as the days of Abraham can do so by paying a visit to some of the interior cities and villages of the Celestial Empire. Excluding Manchuria and Thibet, China is about two-thirds as large as the United States, and possesses all the variety of geographical features, resources, soil, and climate that are found in the same extent of country in other parts of the world. In different parts of China differing environments have produced some variation of type among the people. But these are rather physical than intellectual and moral. In their characteristics, customs, and ways of looking at life we find among them throughout the empire a remarkable homogeneousness.

The best part of China as respects both soil and people is the region of the Yangtse valley, in which the stations of our Southern Presbyterian Mission are located. If my reader will assist me by the vigorous use of his imagination, I will endeavor to show him some of the things to be seen in this region which constitute what may be called our Missionary Environment in China.

For a view of the country we will take our stand on one of the high hills that are found at
A rural scene. frequent intervals along the river banks. From this view point the great valley spreads out before us northward as far as the eye can reach. The alluvial plain lying between the Yangtse and the Hoang-ho on the north is the largest body of valley land to be found in one body anywhere in the world. It is dotted all over with villages, hundreds of them

being in plain view from our hilltop, their adobe houses reminding us, as we watch the yellow-skinned people coming out and going in, of a multitude of great yellow ant hills. Between the villages are the little farms of from one to three acres in extent, naturally fertile, and dressed with liquid fertilizer every afternoon until the air, even our hilltop, is laden with the perfume. In this way their productive power is preserved unimpaired age after age, and, although cultivated with the most archaic implements, the same old wooden plow and pick that the grandson of Noah used, and the fingers of the people, one would judge from the luxuriant growth and dark green color of the vegetation that they are yielding now their very maximum of food in the form of rice and beans and vegetables. These farms are inclosed in a network of canals, which serve to irrigate the crops, and as highways of travel instead of roads. These canals are crowded with house boats and rice boats and foot boats and wood rafts and small junks, driven by sails or pulled by ropes or propelled by a single crooked oar that works on a pivot at the stern, with a motion exactly like that of a fish's tail. They are crossed by frequent bridges of beautiful arched stone work, the best of them many hundreds of years old.

NOACHIAN AGRICULTURE.

We see also a multitude of stone structures of two upright pieces with two transverse pieces at the top, more or less artistically carved and covered with inscriptions. These are memorial arches of those who have given some extraordinary evidence of the virtue which the Chinese have exaggerated into a vice, and which they call "filial piety"; most of them in memory of young women whose betrothed husbands died, and who gave the supreme evidence of filial piety by leaving their own homes and devoting themselves to the service of the mother-in-law that was to have been, or, better still, by joining their betrothed in the spirit world through the door of suicide.

Out in the rice fields and bean patches, and coming and going on the tow-paths, are the people, like the stars of heaven for multitude, not one in a thousand of whom has ever had a dream or an aspiration beyond that of three meals of rice a day, seasoned with a few vegetables and a little salt fish. They are hard featured, curious, unsympathetic, and ungracious, and they flock to a foreigner, and close him in, if he comes anywhere in reach of them, like ants to a piece of bread. One of the least enticing phases of missionary life in China is that you can never get away from these people. They encompass you like a suffocating atmosphere, which one feels at times to be intolerable, but can in nowise escape from. The missionary can only fortify himself against the nervous irritation it produces by nursing visions of the time when, at the end of his eight years' term, he will be able to renew his vitality by breathing once more the air of his native woods and hills. In China he feels at times that one breath of these were worth a king's ransom.

The hill on which we stand and all the surrounding hills are cemeteries, where grave mounds have been accumulating for four thousand years, until they lie as thick almost as they can lie, one against another; and in the mulberry groves, on the canal banks, and on every rising ground in the fields are the heavy wooden coffins, holding the unburied bodies of those who died too poor to afford the luxury of interment, or who have been waiting for months, or perhaps years, for a rascally luck doctor, supported by the family, to find them a fortunate place for burial. It is a grewsome sight, indeed, and no one with a heart in him can witness it without being appalled at the thought of this innumerable multitude, who, while the Christian church, which was commissioned to evangelize them, and whose first reason of existence has been to carry out that commission, has been apparently going on the theory that this was a side issue, a kind of optional duty, or no duty at all, have now gone forever beyond the reach of evangelization. But whoever may have been responsible for these, for those living multitudes, working in those rice fields and coming and going on those tow-paths, the church of to-day that lives contemporary with them is responsible. And if we fail to do what we can to give them the gospel which others have given to us, they also shall die in their sins, but their blood will be required at our hands.

Another important feature of the environment of a missionary in China is the city in which he lives. It is an amazing revelation to one who sees it for the first time of the conditions in which it is possible for human beings to exist and thrive. The Chinese say,

A Chinese city.

"Above is the palace of heaven;
Below are Hangchow and Soochow."

Beautiful for situation is Hangchow, overlooked by rocky hills that duplicate themselves in the clear waters of the West Lake that lies between them and the city. But I enjoyed the privilege of seeing Hangchow in rainy weather, and tasted to the full "the myriad and assorted odors" that rise from its open air sewerage and from the islands of garbage standing up out of pools of a saturated solution of house and kitchen refuse. The main street of the city attains the enormous width of ten feet, but the other streets have an average width of about seven feet.

As one looks up the street the most obtrusive feature in the prospect is the long row of painted and gilded sign boards hanging perpendicularly in front of the shop doors on either side. The houses are usually two-storied, the upper stories being the homes of the people and the lower ones their shops and stores. Across from the upper windows, above the gilded sign boards, ropes are stretched, on which are hung blue cotton trousers and petticoats *galore,* for such an airing as the atmosphere of Hangchow affords. The feature of *"contrast,"* which Mr. Curzon declares to be "the dominant note of Asian individuality," is conspicuously exhibited in the interiors of the shops and stores. In one of them you will see displayed the finest and most richly-colored silks and satins and embroideries in the world. Next door you will see those same silks being woven by the untidiest of women on an old ramshackle loom that creaks and threatens to fall down at every stroke of the batten. Next door to an ivory shop, filled with carvings of such

SUB-LUNARY BLISS.

beauty and delicacy as only Chinese patience and deftness of finger can produce, stands an auction room for unwashed, second-hand clothing, or old rags. Next door to this is a teashop, where a great crowd is gathered to gossip and smoke and gamble with dice and dominoes and fighting crickets, or, with endless chatter and gesticulation, to settle a half-dozen neighborhood quarrels at one time. Opium dens are appallingly frequent, half concealed, but revealing their presence by the emission of their sickening odors. Entering the court of a Buddhist temple, once imposing with its massive timbers and the graduated ascent of its paved approaches, but looking old and dingy now, its glory long departed, we see a few irreverent worshippers performing before the idols, but a great crowd finding entertainment in the performances of the professional story-teller, the juggler, the ventriloquist, or going into or coming out of the booths where every conceivable kind of humbug sideshow is in full blast. If we stay there long we shall find ourselves the greatest side-show of all, and most inconveniently hustled by a crowd whose idea of the dignity of an American citizen is expressed by the greeting, "Where did you come from, you old red-bristled foreign devil?" Out in the little narrow street are the thousands and tens of thousands of the people, jamming and jostling each other in what seems to be, but is not, an impracticable effort to get where they are going, and mingled in what seems to be, but is not, inextricable confusion. An embroidered sedan is loaded with a fat mandarin in silk robes and huge spectacles in tortoise-shell frames, his head bobbing to the motion of his carriers, portentous in his dignity, sublimely unconscious of his absurdity. A creaking wheel-barrow is loaded with three half-naked coolies on one side and three ugly black pigs on the other. The man with the bamboo pole across his shoulders transports by ropes suspended from either end of it every conceivable kind of burden; the traveller's luggage, boxes of merchandise, a movable restaurant, baskets of fresh cabbage and turnips, or of eggs that were once fresh, but, as likely as not, are now far gone in the process of transformation into sulphuretted hydrogen. Most pitiful of all to see are the women hobbling along on their poor little stumps of bound feet, many of them carrying in their arms, or strapped to their backs, from one to three very gaily-dressed, but very dirty-faced and mangy-headed children. Most forlorn and wretched looking, but most useful in their office of street scavengers, are the dogs, as

Street life.

bitterly anti-foreign as the *literati*, but whose superstitious fear of the foreigner is luckily stronger than their hate, so that as we pass along they first rush out with a furious bark and then immediately tuck tail and disappear behind the scenes. Seemingly impossible indeed the situation becomes when, in the midst of all this jam and jumble, a wedding procession going one way meets a funeral procession going the other. But in the long course of their experience the Chinese have wisely come to an understanding about some things, and one of these is as to who has the right of way in the street. And so, incredible as it would seem, they all manage somehow to work their way along and, for anything we ever hear to the contrary, to reach their appointed destinations.

Another thing, of which we are likely to see several in the course of a morning, is a Chinese street quarrel, which differs from all other quarrels as everything Chinese differs from the same thing everywhere else in the world. We observe two men walking side by side engaged in a conversation which grows more and more animated as they proceed. They are probably exchanging opinions as to which of their respective mothers was the most disreputable character in Chinese history. In the space of half a mile they have wrought themselves into a perfect frenzy of rage. Their voices have assumed a tone to which the grating of a shovel on the hearth is music. Finally one of them gives utterance to a sentiment whose vileness of expression and comprehensive breadth of uncomplimentary implication the other cannot hope to rival, whereupon the victor receives the plaudits of the crowd, and the vanquished, having "lost face," retires to grieve over his discomfiture. I was told that these quarrels rarely had any practical results beyond a little harmless pulling of *queues;* but I saw with my own eyes three first-class fisticuffs grow out of them, from which both parties emerged with ugly knots on their heads, and after which I confess that my respect for the Chinese and my hopes for the future of their nation were both considerably enlarged.

Last and most picturesque of all things to be seen in this unique street life is the professional beggar. He is a privileged character, belonging to a guild that protects his interests, for which protection he pays an initiation fee of thirty Mexican dollars.

For an equipment, his face is covered with something worse than ordinary mud. His gray blouse, coming to the knees and frayed at the edges, is stiff with that upon which he has been lying in the street. The part of his person exposed to view is a mass of festering sores. His plan of campaign is to promenade the street, stopping before each shop door, going through various contortions and singing a lugubrious tune, with the view of making himself so disagreeable that no customer will enter the shop while he stands there. When the reluctant shopkeeper at last capitulates by handing him out a cash, the beggar magnanimously raises the siege and moves on to the next shop. Over some shop doors you will see a piece of paper posted, with an inscription to the effect that a fee has been paid to the beggars' guild, in consideration of which that shop-keeper is to have immunity from their solicitations for the space of twelve months.

Time fails to tell of the thousand other things that enter into this amazing and bewildering conglomerate of life in the streets of a Chinese city. It is intensely interesting to one who sees it for the first time and passes on to other scenes. But as a permanent feature of our missionary environment it has a tendency to grow monotonous, and to have the reverse of a tonic effect on missionary nerves.

While the missionaries have their headquarters in the cities, mose of the men, and some of the women, spend much of their time itinerating among the smaller towns and villages. Therefore the available modes of travel become an important feature of their environment.

In Central China the canals take the place of roads, and the principal means of locomotion is the house boat. By carrying your own chair and bed and provisions, and something to read and a supply of pennyroyal and insect powder, one can enjoy life fairly well on a house boat, provided he is not restless on the score of speed. A rice boat is a smaller but speedier craft, and is not to be recommended for a rainy night, such as the one Mr. Paxton and I had for our trip from Sinchang to Soochow, a distance of sixty miles, which we made in sixteen hours. Its covering is a piece of bamboo matting, open at both ends, and usually well supplied with holes, so that you can get full benefit of both the rain and wind. We asked the boatman if he had any bugs on board. He said, "Yes, a couple, but they are family bugs, and will not draw nigh you." "Any mosquitoes?" Answer, "None, if you keep moving; but if you stop, one and a half." Our faith in his assurances was not great, but we did keep moving, and if either the two bugs or the one

Modes of travel.

and a half mosquitoes did draw nigh us, it was while we were asleep, and they did not succeed in waking us.

But when a boat will not take you where you wish to go, then the problem of locomotion becomes like that in the case of the Arkansas traveller, who was told, you remember, that whichever way he went he would not go far before he would wish he had gone some other way. In the region from Tsingkiang-pu north they have the "mule litter" and the famous two-wheeled cart drawn by two mules tandem. Being prevented by want of time from visiting this part of our field, I did not have the opportunity of becoming acquainted by personal experience with these two phases of missionary life. But of the cart I was told that the wheels were usually only partially encompassed by the tire, and that in combination with Chinese roads it is the most perfect device yet framed by man for discovering the exact location of every joint and bone in the human body. The wheel-barrow I had a very small experience of, but, small as it was, I have not since felt the slightest ambition to have it enlarged. The Chinese never lubricate their wheel-barrows, because, they say, "noise is cheaper than oil." You sit on the side of it, with one foot extended in front and the other supported by a rope stirrup. To maintain one's position with dignity when the driver pushes you in his energetic way across a gully, requires the most rapid power of adjustment, as well as forethought and presence of mind. As a device for teaching one to appreciate the luxury of walking, the Chinese wheel-barrow is incomparable. In all the Orient to-day, as in the days of Isaac and Jacob, the donkey is a favorite instrument of transportation. I rode one from Nankin five miles out to the Ming Tombs; but going back I preferred to walk through the broiling sun. Nothing in China is exactly like what the same thing is anywhere else in the world. Whether it be man or animal, the power of heredity working through millenniums of isolation, with no modification from foreign admixture, has developed in every case something that is peculiar to China. The donkey is no exception to this rule. His gait is a rough jog, instead of an easy amble. Our American donkey's bray, we know, is a unique phenomenon in the realm of sound. But that of the Chinese donkey has a quality all its own. It was that, even more than his gait, which distressed me and made me rather walk than ride him. There are no words in English to describe the heart-rendering pathos of it. It was as if an appeal to heaven against

CHINESE EXPRESS.

the cruelty and oppression of ages were at last finding utterance in one long, loud, undulating wail. And when our party of three met another party of six and all nine of the donkeys began at one time to exchange the compliments of the day, one would not have been much astonished to see the dead coming out of those graves on the hillside, mistaking it for an announcement that the day of judgment had come.

The Chinese inn I had experience of had its name inscribed over the door in a character which signified "House of excellent felicity." I have no doubt it was a truthful inscription from a Chinese standpoint, inasmuch as all their ideas of felicity, comfort, and convenience are exactly the reverse of ours. Its guest room had a door opening without a shutter, through which the multitudinous Chinese public were privileged to come in and inspect us and our belongings to their hearts' content. It had a dirt floor, and its walls and roof were frescoed with dirt and cobwebs. It had one piece of furniture, in the shape of a platform in one corner, with a piece of ragged and dirty straw matting spread over it for a bed. Such as it was, Mr. Haden and I were tired enough to take a refreshing nap on it, and then went on our way rejoicing— to leave it behind

Missionary homes. If Shakespeare could have visited in some of the missionary homes in China, he would have had a new conception of a thing to describe as "shining like a good deed in a naughty world." It is the wise policy of most missions to build comfortable western-style houses for their members, and with the nice tableware and *bric-a-brac* ornaments that are to be had in the Orient for a trifle, it is easy with a small outlay to make a sweet and attractive home. Such homes all missionaries ought to have, if possible, to which they may go when their day's work is over and find rest from the nerve strain that one can see must be incident to work in such conditions as I have described. But it is not always possible to have such homes. In opening a new station it usually takes a year, or sometimes two and three years, of negotiating and battling with the authorities to buy a piece of ground. After that comes the experience of the leisureliness with which Oriental carpenters carry out a building contract. During this time the missionary, glad to get a foothold of any kind, contents himself with such accommodations as he may be able to secure. I saw in the outskirts of Kiashing the little three-roomed mud hovel where Dr. Venable and Mr. Hudson spent one whole winter without kindling a fire, except under the dirt oven, because there was nowhere else to kindle it. In the spring Mrs. Venable joined them and lived there several months. Afterwards they moved into a five-roomed hovel, and finally into a native house in the city, where they are now, which has plenty of rooms, but the rooms are so small and dark and unventilated that they cannot be made either sanitary or comfortable. At Wusih I found two missionary families living in ramshackle native houses fronting on a filthy street eight feet wide, with the rear windows hanging over a filthy canal.

But, no matter what kind of exterior surroundings nor interior comforts or discomforts there might be, I found the inside of every missionary home I visited to be a place of brightness and cheer. So far from complaining of their physical hardships are they that, as we know, when they come back to us, lest they might seem to be complaining, they shrink from even telling us the facts of the case. Neither are they unhappy on account of them. They are absorbed and happy in their work. And it is evidently true with most of them that, by emptying their hearts of worldly ambitions and the care for worldly comforts, there has only been made the greater room in them for the blessings of that kingdom which "is not meat and drink, but righteousness and peace and joy in the Holy Ghost." One thing I think they crave to know of us who remain at home—that we cherish them in our hearts, that we remember them in our prayers, and that we are resolved to support them in the work which is ours as well as theirs, and yet is neither ours nor theirs—but Christ's.

In closing this chapter let me say a word concerning the genuine and delightful spirit of brotherhood which I found prevailing among the missionaries of all denominations in China. The denominational lines existing here are reproduced there, as is inevitable. But breaches of spiritual unity growing out of these are rare. Presbyterians of all branches co-operate in work to such an extent as makes them practically one. I cannot speak authoritatively of others in that respect, but I can say that I received everywhere the same welcome into the homes of the missionaries of other churches as of those of my own, and the friendships formed with some of them I count among the most valued trophies brought back from my visit to the **Far East**.

Unity and brotherhood in Chinese missions.

CHAPTER V.

THE MISSIONARY PROBLEM AND WORK IN CHINA.

THE mission of the church in China is not to civilize the Chinese. They have a civilization which is very different from ours, but which is very old and elaborate, and which, having been evolved contemporaneously with their national character, suits them in some respects better than our civilization ever will. Their ancestors were dressing in silks and living under established government and forms of social life ages before ours emerged from the forests of northern Europe, where they dressed in animal skins, ate raw meat for breakfast and roots and berries for dinner, and drank ale at their feasts out of cups made of the skulls of their enemies slain in battle. Our mission is not to introduce among them our western scientific knowledge and the material comforts and conveniences of our western civilization. These will find their way to them in the course of time. But to the extent that they do so in advance of our gospel work, they will constitute an additional barrier instead of an advantage to that work.

The church's business in China is to plant and establish the kingdom of God; and God's instrument for that purpose there and here and every where is the preaching of the gospel.

Preaching in China. In China, just as in this country, the method of preaching needs to be adapted to the character of the audience. I attended a Sunday morning service at Hangchow, where our missionaries have been long enough to have gathered and trained a church of about 150 members. A native woman trained at our Hangchow boarding school presided at the organ. The people sang, with such voices as nature had given them, some of our old church hymns translated into Chinese to the old familiar tunes. The preacher was Mr. Dzen, a native, trained by our mission and ordained as pastor of the church about three years ago. His text was, "Enoch walked with God; and he was not, for God took him." The outline of the sermon, as given me by Rev. G. W. Painter, was, (1), The meaning of walking with God—constant communion. (2), The conditions—faith; love; oneness of mind; a common interest. (3), The results—we shall be afraid of sin; we shall fear nothing else but sin; we shall be with Him at the end and enter with Him into His glory. Though I understood not a word, yet my heart burned within me as I saw in the faces of some of the listeners the radiance of the new life and hope which Christ had brought into their darkened souls; and I felt like saying as I looked over the little church with its plain wooden benches and uncarpeted aisles, "Surely the Lord is in this place; this is none other but the house of God; and this is the gate of heaven."

To reach the outside heathen, other methods have to be employed. The "street chapel" is the chief reliance for this kind of work in the cities. A room is rented that opens on some frequented street and furnished with plain benches and a table and, sometimes, a cabinet organ. The missionary and his native helper go to the chapel and take a stand where they can be seen by the passers-by. The sight of the foreigner or the sound of the organ brings in the crowd, and the missionary begins to talk to any who will listen. He has a hard problem before him. Not only are the ideas he would convey all new and strange to his hearers, but there are no words in their language by which they can be conveyed without endless explanations and circumlocutions. Their language, as well as their thought, is contaminated by centuries of association with idolatry. Their idea of God is of Shangti, whom only the Emperor can worship, and who has no concern for the affairs of ordinary mortals, or of the god of wealth, or the god of war, or of Buddha, whose stone image, with its expressions of idiotic self-complacency, intended to represent the peace of Nirvana, is the central figure in all their temples. Their ideas of truth and morals are all distorted and wrong. They know not what we mean by salvation. Some, as they come in, deposit their burdens and take out their pipes and smoke. Others express audibly their opinion of the "foreign devil," usually the reverse of complimentary. The expressions of countenance are various, but are mostly of suppressed rage or amused curiosity or hopeless stupidity. Into this unpromising soil the missionary and his native helper throw broadcast the good seed of the kingdom. Occasionally one is seen whose face shows that he is wondering if the foreigner really knows of a God who is the friend of the poor and the oppressed and of him that hath no helper. This one will come again, and as he hears over and over again the story of Christ and of his love and power, some day he will learn the joy and peace of believing on him.

This street-chapel preaching is followed up by conversations by the wayside with any they can get to listen to their message, and by the distribution of Bibles and Christian books and tracts.

And so the gospel seed is being sown beside all waters, and the foundations of the kingdom of God are being laid in faith and hope, and little companies of believers are being gathered here and there, and now, after long years of working and waiting, the sowers and the reapers are beginning to rejoice together.

We are also trying to train up a generation of native preachers and workers, and for this purpose we have mission schools. Our Southern *Educational work.* Presbyterian Mission has always occupied conservative ground on the question of schools as an evangelizing agency, and the work at most of our stations being comparatively new, the demand for school work for the children of Christians has been limited. But many "Day Schools" are conducted, where any children who will come and conform to the rules are taught, and where our lady missionaries go and teach them the Bible and the catechism and gospel songs, and then follow them into their homes. In this way they carry the gospel to the Chinese women, many of whom could be reached in no other way. For the training of larger boys and theological students, other missions have established many large high schools and colleges. Our mission as yet has only an industrial boys' school, recently established at Sinchang. At

Hangchow we have a co-operative arrangement with our brethren of the Northern Presbyterian mission, by which we send our boys to their school and they send their girls to ours. Our girls' school at Hangchow has been in operation for thirty years, and now graduates each year a class who have had an eight years' course in which the Bible is the leading text-book. The good that is being accomplished by these graduates in their work as Bible women and church workers, and as the makers of Christian homes, which are the greatest of all needs in China, is incalculable. This and other such schools also serve an indispensable purpose in furnishing our native pastors with educated Christian wives. By a happy coincidence one of the last year's graduates was married while I was at Hangchow to a young man who was about to be sent out several hundred miles into the interior as an evangelist. The ceremony, performed by the old native pastor, was interesting as an illustration of the thoroughness with which the Chinese Christians have been taught to do their work. It opened with a four-versed hymn to the tune to which we sing "The year of jubilee is come"; then followed a long prayer; then a reading of all the passages in the New Testament bearing on matrimony; then a twenty minutes' exhortation; then the pledges; then another hymn dealing very minutely with the subject of reciprocal duties; then another prayer, after which the services closed with the long metre doxology and the benediction. As they started out next day, leaving the little circle of Christian friends they had been living among, which had grown large enough in Hangchow to encourage each other under their trials, to take up their home and work in a community where they would only have each other to lean on, it was pathetic to think of the experiences that inevitably awaited them.

Let it be hoped that they have found in Him whom they serve all needed strength, and that their lives have been blessed by the mutual love which is known in Chinese wedded life only by those who have found it in their mutual love for Christ.[1]

---

[1] Through the kindness of Miss E. C. Davidson and Rev. G. W. Painter we are able to give the following translation in verse of part of the wedding ceremony referred to above.

NATURE OF OBLIGATION AS TOLD BY PASTOR.
1. God has required the vows they take. The husband, though the head,
   Makes promise to revere the wife, nor other woman wed;

Medical work. The work of the *Medical Missionary* is being much emphasized of late years in China as a means of removing the great

> Support and comfort with his love, he doth to her engage,
> When youth and beauty yield their place to ugliness and age.
>
> 2. She too takes pledge that while he lives, her will to his shall bow,
> Or strong or weak, or rich or poor, she will not break her vow.
> Both promise make, should God see fit that one should widowed be,
> Their mutual offspring they'll protect, though to re-wed left free.
>
> ### BRIDAL HYMN.
>
> 1. To show that unity of heart and virtues was God's plan,
> He made the woman from a rib, drawn from the side of man.
> In duties of the marriage state, there should be full accord;
> Whilst mutual honor, trust, and help bring love as their reward.
>
> 2. Assembled thus we all to-day in joyous mood unite,
> By public act to celebrate God's holy nuptial rite,
> In which this bridegroom and his bride, made one out of the twain,
> In body, mind, and will made one, one household shall maintain.
>
> 3. Since they together from henceforth one path through life shall tread,
> May reverence, faith and mutual aid, by mutual love be fed.

hindrance that exists in the hostility of the people to foreigners. Chinese education includes no knowledge of medicine or anatomy or surgery. Consequently they have no physicians of their own to relieve the manifold and pitiful

> May God the Father's constant help secure them lasting peace;
> Whilst misery, woe, and carking care from them forever cease.
>
> 4. O Heavenly Father! ever grant thine unremitting care;
> May clashing discord never jar this God-united pair:
> We further crave thy guardian care for ages yet to come;
> May their descendants serve thee, Lord; nor to thy praise be dumb.
>
> 5. May blessings from a Father's hand upon their home descend,
> And grace profound in man and wife in like proportions blend.
> Deep reverence for their Saviour-Lord, O Holy Ghost, inspire!
> Whilst filial service all through life their single hearts shall fire.
>
> 6. What things we crave, O Father dear! wilt not thou deign bestow?
> That man and wife—unsevered pair—to ripe old age may grow,
> Together bear the ills of life, together share its joy,
> And after death in heaven's bright halls together find employ.
> —*Translated from the Chinese by the Rev. G. W. Painter.*

forms of disease that spring from the conditions in which they live. In this case the work of the medical missionary answers in part the same purpose as the miracles of healing wrought by Christ and his apostles. Many large hospitals have been established, which bear their constant and powerful witness to the beneficent character of Christianity, and become centres from which gospel light is distributed by those who have been taught, as well as healed, in them.

Our mission has only one hospital, the one recently built at Soochow at a cost of $10,000, the gift of one man who chose the wise plan of giving his money to this beneficence while he lived, and who now lives to see and enjoy the fruit of his Christian generosity. But we have eight medical missionaries working at our various stations with such facilities as they can command, and who last year (1897) ministered to about 40,000 patients. I spent a morning with Dr. Venable at Kiashing and saw the little room ten feet square with a dirt floor which he called his "hospital," in which he was treating a poor fellow with a broken thigh, who already seemed to have the death pallor on his face, but who, by the blessing of God on the doctor's skill, came through with a good recovery. Mrs. Venable and her sister, Miss Talbot, spent the morning in the dispensary, applying antiseptic ointments and bandages to all kinds of horrible sores and ulcers which the people contract from drinking their canal water, and from standing barelegged in the rice fields; and in dispensing medicines prescribed by the doctor. In addition to the regular prescriptions, every patient was furnished, for obvious purposes, a small jar of sulphur and lard. Some of the cases they handled I scarcely had the nerve to look at. Yet they were doing their work cheerfully and happily, finding their compensation in the luxury of doing good.

In serious surgical cases a written contract is made with the patient's family, in which they assume all responsibility for the result. It is often necessary also to perform the operation in public to prevent scandalous stories as to what barbarous things the barbarian doctor does with his patient. Even with these precautions it is often possible that a fatal result might lead to a riot. Dr. Worth told me that he once administered chloroform to a woman while a crowd of her friends stood by with an expression on their faces which plainly meant, "now, if she does not come back to life we will make short work with you." For a moment her pulse did stop beating and he thought his time had come, but, fortunately, it returned again, and the operation was a brilliant success. Shortly afterwards another crowd brought him a dead woman and insisted that he should try to restore her to life. These are a few sample illustrations of the medical mission work. And God is blessing the noble and self-denying labors of our missionary doctors and of the women that assist them, so that through them thousands of bitter enemies are being turned into friends, and the doors are being opened through which the missionary preacher can find his way to the ministry of souls.

CHAPTER VI.

HINDRANCES.

WHEREVER the church has been established in the world it has had to meet and overcome many obstacles. But nowhere else in the world to-day do we encounter such a combination of obstacles as in China, growing out of the peculiar character, the peculiar institutions, and the peculiar superstitions of the people.

Characteristics. Physically, the Chinese are very much superior to any other people in the Orient; and if not superior, they are certainly not inferior intellectually. As between China and Japan, there was no dispute on that point so late as a half century ago. Up to that time all the civilization that Japan had had been derived from China; the Chinese sages, Confucius and Mencius, because she had none of her own, were her teachers in philosophy and morals, and the Chinese classics were the text-books in her schools.

China is behind Japan to-day because her pride and conservatism have beaten back the impact of our western civilization, which Japan, having been long accustomed to receive from others, has admitted and embraced. If these can be broken down and her students induced to apply themselves to the acquisition of modern knowledge, it will not be long until their plodding industry will have placed them in the front rank among the scholars of the world. In social morality and reliability, they compare favorably with other Orientals, and though much addicted to lying, as all Orientals are, the difference between them and some Americans in that respect is not greater than it should be, considering that China is heathen and America is supposed to be a Christian land. Many of their characteristic traits are those which, under the regenerating influence of Christianity, would go into the make-up of a great and noble people. They are sober-minded, industrious, enterprising, peaceable, and law-abiding. But they have two outstanding traits which, until they are greatly modified in some way, will prevent them from becoming a great and noble people, and cause them to be in the future as they have been in the past, the most difficult of all people to reach with the gospel. These are their monumental and unparalleled conceit and their preposterous and paralyzing conservatism. If there is more hope of a fool than of one wise in his own conceit, what hope is there of a nation of people who call their country "The Great, Pure Kingdom," "The Flowery Kingdom," "The Celestial Empire"; who look on themselves and all their belongings as absolutely perfect, and on the most refined and cultivated westerner that comes to them as a poor, ignorant barbarian from the far-off fringes of the world, worthy only of their enlightened scorn?

Their conservatism has its roots in their ancestor worship, which leads them to resent any suggestion of improvement from any quarter as an insult to these ancestors. The way it works will appear from the following illustration:

Old and New Shanghai. The first thing that one, going from this direction, sees of China is the city of New Shanghai. It is a fine, modern city, with numerous factories, run by modern machinery and lighted by electricity. A wide boulevard on the river front is lined with a magnificent row of three and four-story business houses, of brick and stone. There are several squares of two and three-story brick flats for residences, furnished with water and gas and all modern conveniences. There is one of the most beautiful of pleasure gardens, with its green turf and foliage plants and flowers and ornamental trees, and red chairs and settees, where the tired merchants come of evenings and sit and smoke, and drink in the fresh ocean breeze; and graveled walks, where the young people promenade and tell their story of love and adventure, to the accompaniment of moonlight and sweet music.

One would suppose that all these desirable things of our western civilization, carried out there and put right before the eyes of the Chinese, would excite their admiration and awaken in them a desire to have the same things. Let us see. Passing through a gate in the wall that separates New Shanghai from Old Shanghai, we find ourselves in a typical Chinese city, said to make about the least pretension to decency and cleanliness of any city in the Empire. Ask the people of Old Shanghai if they would not like to have clean streets, and houses with grass plots around them, and marble-fronted stores and a pleasure garden. They answer, "No, our ancestors for thousands of years have dispensed with such things, and shall we set ourselves up as wiser and better than they?" I was told that the municipality of New Shanghai did offer to extend its waterworks, free of charge, to Old Shanghai, in the hope of thereby preventing the pestilences that originate in the foulness of its streets and canals. They responded by sending a committee to investigate the water that was offered them. The committee went back and reported that they did not like it. "It has no body to it," they said, "like the water of our canals. It has neither taste nor smell." Whether this story be true or apocryphal, it exactly illustrates the attitude of China, not only to clean water and western comforts and conveniences, but to the western man himself and every thing he brings with him, Christianity not excepted.

<small>National evolution.</small> The process of national evolution has had a long time to work itself out in China along the lines projected by the ancient fathers, and the result is as though the "God of this world" had been the presiding genius of it, and had been given unlimited opportunity to do his worst in the way of making China hopelessly inaccessible to the gospel.

In government there has been evolved a *patriarchal despotism*, in which "the beautiful sentiment of filial piety" binds all the people to abject and unquestioning submission to "the powers that be," from the Emperor down to the father of the family, the elder brother and the mother-in-law.

The governors of provinces and the magistrates of cities and towns are taken from an official class composed of those who have passed a series of examinations in the Confucian classics. Hundreds of thousands of the young men of China go up every year to the provincial capitals to compete for the degree that puts them in the line of promotion. These are the so-called "Literati," whose education we might suppose would make them the friends of light and progress. But, as a matter of fact, it only fortifies them in their lofty scorn of anything more modern than Confucius. And besides, being either officials or expectant officials, all their personal hopes and interests are bound up in the system that now exists, and so they present a solid front of opposition to anything in the shape of reform or change. The few who, by luck, or influence or bribery, reach the coveted goal of office receive only nominal salaries from the government, which they are expected to supplement by such means as opportunity may throw in their way. This opportunity they find in pilfering the public revenues that pass through their hands, in exacting bribes from all litigants, and in torturing accused criminals until the last possible cash has been extracted from them as the price of their release. If they should become Christians, they would have to give up their handsome incomes from these wages of iniquity. They would also have to resign their offices, be-

SEEKING JUSTICE.

cause their official duties require them to engage in idolatrous rites and ceremonies. No wonder then that the gospel finds in the officials and *literati* of China its bitterest opponents, and any one can see that if Satanic inspiration had been invoked to devise an official system that would present the greatest possible obstacle to our Christian missions, he could not improve upon the one that now exists.

In the *industrial sphere* there has been developed a guild system that holds all trades and professions in an iron grip. Every merchant or artisan must belong to the guild, or be boycotted. Even the beggars and thieves have guilds, the initiation fee to the beggars' guild in Soochow being $30 (Mexican). And if anyone attempts to practice this honored profession without being a member of the guild, a committee is appointed, who take their stand on a bridge in the dusk of the evening and, as the offender passes by, a knock on the head and a toss into the canal bring his career to a speedy and inglorious termination. The guilds as such are taxed to support the temples and the idol processions. When one becomes a Christian, he will no longer wish to help support idolatry. He must therefore break with the guild and become an industrial outcast. If we had such a system to contend with in this country, it would certainly diminish the number of our professed converts, even though it might improve their quality. The religions of China are said to be Buddhism, Tauism, and Confucianism in the form of ancestral worship. But these have long been boiling in a pot together until they have lost their distinctive characteristics, and the people have them hopelessly confused. I saw at Shanghai a Tauist priest conducting Confucian worship in a Buddhist temple. The residuum from the old religions is a system of demon worship, which is a veritable reign of terror, and is the source of untold misery as well as of mental and spiritual degradation. The people believe that earth and air and water are filled with malignant spirits that pursue them night and day, and the effort to propitiate them, or to cajole them, or to dodge them, is the aim of nine-tenths of their religious observances. Departed ancestors are kept in good humor by burning paper money and clothes and horses and other conveniences at their tombs, which, being etherealized in smoke, become available for use in the spirit world. The odor of savory viands set on tables around their tombs is also thought to be necessary for their nourishment and gratifying to their spiritual olfactories.

Religions.

The spirits of wind and water are fortunately supposed to be able to travel only in straight lines. Hence you will see rectangular brick pillars built opposite a man's front gate, a little larger than the opening. The spirits coming in that direction butt against this pillar and are thrown to the ground. When they get up and start again, they must still go in a straight line, and so their entrance into the premises is prevented. Every tiled roof has an upward curve at each corner. This is to give any vagrant spirit who might be sliding down the comb of the roof a slant upward as he leaves it, so that he will not come gliding through the door or window of some adjoining house. Fear of the consequences which may come to them through the ill will of these ancestral and other spirits if the honors due them are in any way neglected, a fear that often abides long after the mind has been emancipated from belief in them, is one of the hardest things to be overcome with those who are brought to consider the claims of the gospel.

Then there is the gambling curse, almost universally prevalent, and the opium curse, the smell of which is in all the air and the pallor of it on millions of faces, and many other things of which there is no more time to speak, which, taken all together, make up a situation which would seem to render the evangelization of China an utterly impracticable and hopeless undertaking. It is no wonder that men of the world, looking at it from their worldly standpoint, have so regarded it, and have told us that the money and the lives of the men and women devoted to this work are being simply thrown away. Are they? Let us see.

Results. Robert Morrison went as the first Protestant missionary to China in 1807. When he died, in 1834, he had only a half-dozen professed converts to show as the result of his life work. And some, who forgot that foundations have to be laid before a building can be erected, said that he had thrown his life away. But to-day there is a Protestant church in China with about 80,000 communing members, more than half of whom have been added in the last eight years, and five-sixths of them in the last twenty years. The rate of progress steadily increases as the number of trained natives increases who are prepared to preach the gospel to their own people. The number is already great enough to show that human impossibilities and insurmountable obstacles do not count as such when they come into collision with the power of God in the gospel.

Character of native Christians. But, looking to the future of the church in China, the most important question is not how many native Christians are there, but what kind of Christians are they?

There are some of all classes, but most of them are of the poorer classes, as was the case with the church which Christ and the apostles established. Some have come in from wrong motives, hoping for employment, or the foreigners' help in law-suits, or some material advantage. This cannot be always prevented, although the greatest possible pains are taken to prevent it. The great majority of them, however, have come in expecting on the worldly side just what they found—disinheritance, boycotting, abandonment of family and friends, and a thousand forms of persecution. Many are as to knowledge mere babes in Christ. In symmetry of Christian character we cannot rightly expect of them what we do of those who have been born in the midst of Christian environments and reared in Christian homes. But I bear witness of what I saw among them, that in simple childlike faith, in zeal for the cause they have espoused and in the patient endurance of persecution many of them have been, and are now, showing the spirit of the Christians of apostolic days.

In our little church at Soochow there is a native preacher by the name of Mr. Leu. When Dr. Davis was negotiating for the land on which our hospital is built, Mr. Leu offered his services to act as native "middleman" in the purchase. The local magistrate is bitterly opposed to the foreigners acquiring property, and in a similar transaction some years ago the magistrate in charge revenged himself on the native who took part in it by arresting him on some false accusation and throwing him into prison, where he lay for several years. This was the probable fate of Mr. Leu. But he did not hesitate on that account. He went out and found an old man and initiated him into the care of his home, so that the old man could manage things for him during the indefinite time that he expected to lie in prison. He did not seem to be conscious that he was doing anything heroic. But, knowing as he did the barbarities of a Chinese prison, it seems to me that in this matter this man was a Christian hero, of the very same spirit with him who said in the olden time, "I am ready, not to be bound only, but also to die at Jerusalem, for the name of the Lord Jesus."

I am thankful to say that the land for the hospital was secured, and, by the kind providence of God, Mr. Leu was saved from the fate

MR. LEU AND FAMILY.

which he and his friends anticipated for him. And this was the man who stood up in the congregation in Soochow one Sunday morning, in last October, and responded to my address, asking me to carry back to the home church a message of love and gratitude from him and his people for sending them the gospel, and to ask your prayers, "not," he said, "that we may not have to suffer persecution, for we read in this Bible that those who will live godly in Christ Jesus must suffer persecution, but that God will always be with us in future as He has been in the past, and give us His grace to make us faithful unto death."

For my part, I felt like sitting at that disciple's feet, that I might learn more of the spirit of Christ. And this is not a solitary case, but there are many like him among the Christians of China who are ready any hour to give the supreme test of their fidelity and love. And we have now reached a stage in our work when we are no longer compelled as Judson was when asked what was the prospect in Burmah, to point to the Bible and say, "Bright as the promises of God." We can point to the promises, and also to the actual visible results, so large and so rapidly increasing in quantity, and some of them so magnificent in quality, and say, "We are not ashamed of the gospel of Christ, for it is the power of God unto salvation"—even in China. The power of God will not fail us. He is in China to-day working mightier miracles than that by which the walls of Jericho were thrown down. The native Christians there will not fail us. They have already been tried in the fire and their faith found to be of the quality that is imperishable. The Protestant missionaries there will not fail us. The church has never had a nobler or more self-denying band of workers than they are. The only cloud on the horizon is that the church at home seems at present unwilling to give them the support and re-enforcement they need in the ever-widening work that opens up before them.

CHAPTER VII.

THE COUNTRY AND PEOPLE OF KOREA.

IN the month of October, 1897, I watched a Korean sunset from the top of a hill near the village of Kunsan, on the southwestern coast. The sombre effect of the brown rocks of the coast cliffs and of the little islands in the bay, and of the brown grass on the hills, was only intensified by the green of a few scattering, scrubby pines. The golden clouds and the scarlet waters were as still as if they had been painted on a canvas. There was hardly a breath of movement in the air, and the only things in all the landscape that seemed possessed of waking life were myself and a few geese and ducks that were floating lazily out on the bosom of the ebbing tide.

The scene was typical of that far-away little kingdom which we insist on calling Korea, but which the natives call Chosön,—the "Land of the Morning Calm." It was indeed a land of "calm," of industrial, social, political, religious, and every other kind of calm, from immemorial days of old until about twenty-five years ago, when its quietude began to be disturbed by visitors from the West, firing salutes from their battleships in its harbors and asking the privilege of extending to it the benefits of their protection and trade. In recent years it has become the passive but interested subject of much interesting diplomacy among these visitors, especially those representing Russia and England. Russia's interest was to dominate Korea, not for the sake of any immediate value to her of the trade and resources of the country, but with the view of possessing herself of one of the fine harbors, notably that of Port Lazareff, on the eastern coast, both as the long-coveted outlet for her trans-Siberian trade, and as a place where she might gradually assemble a navy that would enable her to cope with England in the waters of the Far East. England's interest was to frustrate the designs of Russia. Now that Russia has secured her outlet in Port Arthur on the China coast, it is noticeable that she is not interesting herself in Korea to the same extent as formerly. That she may cease to do so entirely is a consummation devoutly to be wished, for many reasons, but especially in the interest of our Protestant missionary work. Our country has as yet had no political interests in Korea at all and has been concerned in none of her recent political troubles. For this reason our missionaries are more welcome there than those of any other country.

The Korean peninsula stretches from the southern boundary of Manchuria and the northeast boundary of China southward, between the thirty-third and forty-fourth degrees of north latitude. It is traversed through its whole length by a range of mountains that sends off frequent spurs in both directions to the sea. These geographical conditions give it a climate which, excepting the rainy season, which lasts about two months in summer, is simply superb. The scenery is picturesque and the valleys are fertile, and both would be more so but for the utter denudation of the hills by the peasants in search of fuel, which is in more senses than one "the burning question" in all the Orient. In the north there is said to be some fine timbered lands, but in the south, where I travelled, there is only an occasional patch of scrubby pines, reserved by the government, and twisted into every conceivable shape by the winds.

Geography and climate.

As in China, the hills are all cemeteries, though not so thickly populated with the dead as the hills of China. High up on their sides and tops are the well-kept grassy mounds, the graves of the well-to-do, generally marked by stone slabs, and regularly visited and put in order once a year.

Lower down are the unburied bodies of the peasants, wrapped in coffins of rice straw, and in the case of children, mounted on sticks or swung from the boughs of trees to keep them from being eaten by the foxes. This objectionable custom springs, perhaps, not so much from indifference to the bodies of their dead as from the fear that their burial before the proper place had been selected by the geomancer would bring disaster to the family.

The staple productions are rice and beans and millet, as condiments to which a variety of salads, turnips, and red pepper are grown. I found the native food uneatable, for reasons both of taste and of sentiment. Unless by special order, the rice and beans are cooked together and then seasoned with pepper until the whole mixture is red. A flavor as of ancient dish water exhales from the mixture when hot. If meat is served, one knows not whether it was killed or died a natural death. Most likely the latter, but if killed, the method is usually by strangling, so as not to lose the weight of the blood. One can venture on the fish, because they have no blood, and we ourselves have learned no better as yet than to let the fish we eat die a natural death.

The chief reliance of the missionary and traveller in Korea for food for some time to come must be on canned goods from San Francisco.

With somewhat better conditions of travel and forage, Korea would be the sportsman's paradise. In the autumn the grassy hills are thick with pheasants, and the rice fields with ducks and geese. Small deer and leopards are plentiful in many places, and tigers scarcely inferior to the Royal Bengal make themselves altogether too familiar around some of the villages for the comfort of the Koreans, who are not supplied with the proper munitions of war to cope with them. Some of the natives have old match-lock rifles with which they shoot ducks and geese sitting, provided they will sit long enough after the native gets a bead on them for the old string fuse to burn up to the powder in the flash pan. With such weapons they cannot aspire to shoot game on the wing, but they express their sportsman's instinct by shouts of delight when they see a foreigner bring down a flying goose with a breech-loader.

Game.

If one wishes to describe the conditions of interior travel in Korea he may use any derogatory word our language contains, or any combination of them, without the slightest danger of exaggeration.

Travel.

There are no made roads and no canals to take the place of them as in China. Short journeys may be made in comfort in a sedan chair. But for long journeys, requiring much weight and bulk of luggage, the favorite instrument of transportation is that unique, natural phenomenon, the Korean pony. This animal possesses the general contour of a horse, but in other respects he is peculiar, and peculiar to Korea. He is very small, but is a marvel of strength and endurance. His face is very much dished, and his face expresses his character, which attains perhaps the maximum of combined obstinacy and ferocity possible to horse flesh. Not wishing to do him injustice, I have made comparison with the observations of other travellers and find them substantially the same as my own. Mrs. Bishop pronounces him to be "among the most salient features of Korea," and says that, though she dearly loved horses, she was not able in a whole month to establish any friendly relations with the one she rode. Mr. Gale, in his "Korean Sketches," tells us that he exists in three stages of development. He grows wild on a certain island, where a number of them are lassoed each year and taken to the royal stables. Here he spends his palmy days. When he begins to look shaggy and sheepy

READY TO START.

from age he is taken out and used as a pack pony for the government. This is the second stage, during which he develops ringbone, rawback, stringhalt, spavin and heaves. Then he is purchased by a dealer, who keeps him to hire to foreigners. But through all these stages his spirit remains unbroken, and while he lives he will yield the palm to no other living horse in the weight he will carry and the distance he will travel in a day. My experience of him was on a journey of 175 miles from Seoül to Chunju, in company with Mr. Eugene Bell, of our mission, which we accomplished in five days. The *impedimenta* for this journey for each pony were two good boxes of provisions and utensils, a valise, a folding cot, a comfort, a pillow and blanket, besides the rider. Mounted on them, on top of all this luggage, with no support for back or feet or hands, our appearance was no less picturesque than our situation was helpless and uncomfortable. But I soon learned the secret of this mode of travel. It is to ride until your back is so tired you cannot possibly endure it longer; then walk till you are so wearied that any change will be a relief; then mount your pony again. I found also that in crossing streams on arched dirt bridges two feet wide, walking was preferable to riding, and also when the road was the narrow bank between two flooded rice fields. Our resting place at night was the Korean inn, if resting place it could be called. Its guest room opens on the enclosed back yard of the premises, the rendezvous of our ponies and of the landlord's dogs and pigs and chickens, and furnished with earthenware jars, the receptacle of whatever can be made available to improve the productiveness of the rice fields. The room is nine feet by six, with a raised floor heated hot by a flue under it, and no opening except the small door by which we enter. Our alternative was to open the door to the incursion of crawling and hopping parasites from without, or to close it and take our chances with the stifling air within. We unwisely chose the latter, with the result that, after a brief nap, I awoke in a nightmare, dreaming that I was buried alive. We then tried it with the door open, and were weary enough to bid defiance to the animal creation, large or small, to disturb our slumbers. But just then there appeared on the scene a Buddhist monk with his band of helpers, trying to exorcise a demon from a neighboring house where there was small-pox, beating gongs and blowing something that sounded like a Scotch bagpipe, and singing tunes, the like of which I never heard before, and hoped I might never hear again. This benevolent enterprise was kept up till two o'clock in the morning, with what success we never learned, as we rose at half-past four and proceeded on our journey. I indulged the hope on starting that after a day or two we would toughen to our experiences and find them less intolerable. This might have been the case, but for the development of a Korean carbuncle on the hip joint. As it was, at the end of the journey I was more than satisfied to be simply alive. Such is the romance and luxury of missionary itinerating in Korea. And at present much the larger part of male missionary life there is itinerating.

The port of entry to Korea from the west is Chemulpo, in whose so-called harbor the tide rises from twenty-five to forty feet.

Cities and villages.

When the tide recedes, the bottom for a mile out is left entirely bared, leaving junks and small steamers resting on the ooze till another tide comes in to float them. Fifty-six miles from Chemulpo up the river Han, and three miles from the river, lies Seoül, the capital of the country.

It was up this stretch of river that, in 1872, Commodore Rogers and Capt. Schley and Ensign Mitchell Chester, now captain of the gunboat Cincinnati, attempted to navigate the old

Monocacy, the "Noah's Ark" of our Asiatic squadron, to avenge the murder of the crew of an American schooner that was wrecked on the northwestern coast. They had the usual experience of those who attempt this journey, whether by gunboat, steam launch, or junk, of finding themselves stuck in the mud a few miles up the river, and they had to take to the land to accomplish their purpose. This they did, with difficulty however, for the Koreans fought desperately from behind their rock forts on the mountain cliffs. But their string-fuse *jingals* were too long in going off, and their old Chinese brass cannon all went off at once, leaving them helpless at the hands of the Americans, who shot and bayonetted together about six hundred of them. The American loss was Lieut. McKee and two marines killed, and eight wounded. Except in the display of American pluck it was an unworthy episode, which the Koreans seem happily to have forgotten.

In respect of population, Scoül ranks as one of the great cities of the Far East, containing about 250,000 inhabitants. But in any other respect than population it hardly deserves the name of a city at all. It has no arts nor manufactures worth speaking of. As to trade, Mrs. Bishop says truly that "it is the commercial centre of a people whose ideas of commerce are limited to huckstering transactions." It has no two-storied houses, except a few built by foreigners, even the royal palaces being of but one story. A few of the houses are built of wood, and covered with tiles, but the vast majority of them are simply mud huts with three small rooms, covered with thatched straw. Korea is a country of villages, however, rather than of large cities, and every village is like every other village, a collection of these mud huts, scattered all over the country at an average distance of from three to five miles.

The streets of cities and villages alike are narrow alleys with open gutters on either side, filled with malodorous sewage, in which naked children play as though they were clear mountain streams. It must be said for the city of Seoül, however, that its street odors are less pungent and stifling than those of a Chinese city, and it is distinguished by three fine boulevards, fifty yards wide, and smoothly graveled, which shine in the prospect from the city wall with a conspicuousness increased by contrast with their surroundings. Thronged with pedestrians of both sexes, all dressed in white, and topped off with such a variety of headgear as the ingenuity of no other people on earth has invented, every profession, trade, or grade of social life being distinguished by its own peculiar hat, these boulevards present an appearance that can hardly be matched for picturesqueness in the street life of the world. Another unique feature of Korean street and road life is the endless procession of bulls, covered with enormous loads of grass or twigs, until only the face and lower part of the limbs are visible, led by a ring in the nose, perfectly docile, and politely turning aside without suggestion from their drivers to give the right of way to the passing traveller.

Approaching Korea from the west, about thirty miles from the mainland we pass through an archipelago of small rocky islands.

The people.

Here we get our first view of the natives, cruising among these islands in their little brown junks, which they have loaded from the hulk to the top of the mast with bundles of grass gathered on the islands for fuel. Our first observation of them is that they are all dressed from top to toe in white cotton. This costume is universal, and indicates one of their most interesting national peculiarities.

Their white dress is a badge of national mourning. In former years when any member of the royal family died, the nation was required to wear white for twelve

A nation of mourners.

months. In later and more troublous times, the occasion for the white dress came so often, and the expense and trouble of changing to it was so burdensome, that they adopted it as the permanent national costume, so as to be in readiness for the emergency as it might arise.

When any member of a family dies, the family is expected to go into mourning from one to three years, according to the nearness of the relationship. The badge of this family mourning for the men is an enormous bamboo hat, of conical shape, coming down over the face and shoulders like an umbrella, and signifying that "Heaven is angry with the mourner, and does not wish to look upon his face." During this mourning period it is contrary to custom for the man to marry. And so it often happens that, by a succession of family bereavements one finds himself carried on past youth and middle life, even to old age, and condemned at last to an enforced permanent celibacy. This is the most deplorable of calamities to an Oriental, because it means that he shall have no male posterity to care for his grave and to worship his departed spirit. Furthermore, with the Koreans it entails the disadvantage that an unmarried man, though he should live to ninety years of age, is always regarded and treated as a "boy," entitled to no respect, and always to be addressed in the "lowest talk." It is in their funeral processions that mourning is reduced to the finest of the fine arts. The pall-bearers carry the coffin hoisted on poles, singing a woeful dirge, and ever and anon turning and retracing their steps, or stopping and marking time, as though they could not go upon their melancholy errand. Much of this mourning, of course, is mere form and conformity to custom. But perhaps there is no nation of people more afflicted with real sorrows than the Koreans, and none therefore with a deeper need of, and a stronger claim on, that gospel which offers the only real comfort that this world knows to the mourning sons of men.

On landing at Chemulpo, a boy about fourteen years of age took my two steamer trunks and a valise and piled them on a wooden rack, which they call a "chee-kai," and getting under the burden, walked with it with apparent ease up a steep hill about two hundred yards to the hotel. Another, of about the same size, took a cooking stove on his back and did the same thing. It is said to be not uncommon for a grown man to carry in this way for several miles a burden of four hundred pounds. A countryman will carry one hundred and fifty pounds of rice on his back from the point of the penin-

Burden-bearers.

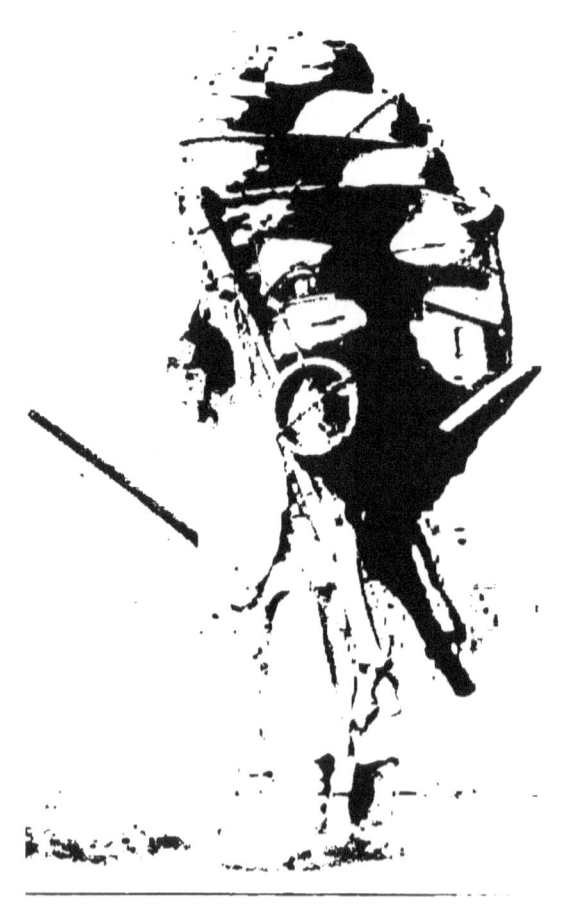

TRANSPORTATION BY CHEE-KAI.

sula two hundred miles to the capital, and carry back the same weight of baled cloth. A child five years old will play all day with one a year old strapped to his back. In this way the loin muscles are trained from infancy for their work. Everywhere one goes throughout Korea he sees these human beasts of burden stooping under their loads; and one thinks of the other burdens they carry, of unforgiven sins and uncomforted sorrows, and wonders if there might not be for them a special meaning and a peculiar sweetness in the Saviour's invitation to those that "labor and are heavy laden." May the day soon come when all of them shall hear it, and when all of them who will may come to Him and find rest for both body and soul. To-day, in all the Orient, the cheapest of all things is man. Only in the Christ we preach to him will he find again the value of his manhood as well as the supply of his spiritual needs.

Characteristics. Mr. Curzon mentions as one of the Oriental traits which he found everywhere in his travels, from India to the farthest east, "a statuesque and inexhaustible patience, which attaches no value to time, and wages an unappeasable warfare against hurry."

Absence of hurry. Perhaps it is among the Koreans that this trait has attained its most extreme development. I encountered it among my very first experiences in a way not soon to be forgotten. Attempting to go by the little river steamer from Chemulpo to Seoül, we had the usual experience a few miles up the river of finding ourselves deposited on a sandbank. Korean sail and row boats were everywhere in evidence, but none of them could be persuaded to attempt the passage against an adverse tide. After some hours delay a Japanese *sampan* was sighted coming down the river, loaded with Koreans on their way to a market at some place about two days' journey distant. We proposed to the Japanese boatman to unload his Koreans and take us up the river for a consideration of ten dollars. After some parley, they consented to the arrangement and took their places on the river bank, where they sat like sea fowls, perfectly quiet and content, for eighteen hours until the boatman returned. At Seoül we had to hire some ponies, and having but one day in which to see the sights of the capital, we sought to expedite this business transaction as much as possible. Several times the dealer brought us ponies which he knew we would reject on account of their dilapidated condition. Each time Mr. Bell would shout at him, pointing to the front gate, "Go—go, go fast, and bring us the right kind of ponies," using all the additional hurrying words that his Korean vocabulary suitable to a missionary contained. When the trade was finally closed, we found that we had been engaged in it exactly five hours. They will not be in a hurry, and woe be to the fast-going western man that goes out there and tries to make them be. The lines in which Mr. Rudyard Kipling describes the fate of the Englishman trying to do the same thing in India will also be true of him. Says Mr. Kipling:

> "It is not good for the Christian's health
> To hustle the Aryan brown,
> For the Christian riles and the Aryan smiles,
> And he weareth the Christian down.
> And the end of the fight is a tombstone white,
> With the name of the late deceased,
> And the epitaph drear, 'A fool lies here,
> Who tried to hustle the East.'"

The Koreans are similar to both Chinese and Japanese in feature and physique, but in some respects are different from both. In color they are a lighter shade of yellow than either, and their hair is frequently of a russet brown color. They are of good size, but much deteriorated physically from various blood diseases that originate in their unsanitary mode of living. They are very hospitable and polite, and, as compared with Chinese and Japanese, quite amiably disposed towards foreigners. The masses are wretchedly ignorant, as must be the case under such a government as they have, but a few of them who have gone abroad and been educated in this country and in Europe, have demonstrated that they are by no means deficient in native capacity. Men like Dr. Philip Jaisohn, editor of the Korean Independent newspaper, and Mr. Yun, a distinguished graduate of our Vanderbilt University, and afterwards Minister of Education in the government of Korea, both of them also bold and outspoken Christians, are men who, for character and intelligence would be a credit to any country. Any country that can produce such men as these is a country worth trying to save.

The government of Korea is one of the old paternal despotisms that have been the immemorial curse of Asia. The king, recently advanced to the dignity of Emperor, although he is a person of very great international insignificance, is none the less the object of superstitious veneration by his own people, who call him "the Son of Heaven," to whom his will is law, and who belong to him, body and soul, in fee simple. Local government is in the hands of a hereditary ruling class called Yangbans, in whom we find the *apotheosis* of the gentleman of elegant leisure. Being quite numerous, not all of them can be in office at any one time. But those who are in know not how soon they may be out, and those who are out hope soon to be in, and so they stand by one another, extending and receiving favors as their mutual needs and abilities demand and make practicable. The first principle of Yangban political economy is that no one of his class is ever under any circumstances to do any work. Even to light his own pipe would require an altogether unbecoming amount of exertion, and so he smokes a pipe with a stem so long that he must needs have a servant to light it for him. When out of pocket, he pays long visits to his friends, using and abusing the hospitality which it would be a disreputable breach of ancient custom not to extend.

The second principle of their political economy is that no one of the common people is to be allowed to accumulate property. A new gate, a repaired roof, or any visible sign of improved circumstances is liable to prove the occasion of arrest. The charge may be that the man was heard to speak disrespectfully of his mother. No matter what the charge is, once in the magistrate's prison he stays there, being "bambooed" every morning at sunrise, until all the available money of the family has been paid in as the price of his release. The consequence of this system is, of course, the universal poverty of the common people, who not only have no incentive for trying to accumulate property, but the strongest possible incentive for not doing so. There is an average grade of cruelty and oppression on the part of these officials that is expected, and if one does not exceed it, perhaps the people may build a monument to him when he dies, inscribed with the praise of his moderation and virtue. But sometimes when one goes too far in excess of this average grade, and becomes intolerable, the people give way to their outraged sense of justice and put him to death. The fact that they have done this occasionally to individuals gives reason to hope that they may some day have enough manhood developed in them to rise up and destroy the system, and thus open the way for the possible splendid future of their beautiful and fertile land.

If it be possible for the social and domestic life of a people to be arranged on a more unde-
<small>Social and domestic life.</small> sirable basis than that of the Koreans, I am unable to imagine what that arrangement would be. Polygamy in the technical sense does not prevail. Only one legal wife is recognized. But every man takes to him-

IRONING CLOTHES.

self as many "secondary" wives as he can provide room for and support. In order that they may be serviceable in all kinds of work, the women of the peasantry have the freedom of the streets and roads and rice fields; but those of the upper classes live in the back rooms of their little houses in total seclusion. The unwillingness of the Koreans to let their women be seen leads to one of the many reversals of our customs, in that men going on pleasure escapades go in the day time, while the women go on theirs at night. When a woman must go out in the day time she goes in a closed chair. The coolies take the chair and set it down in the back yard and retire. When the "coast is clear," the woman comes out and takes her seat in the chair and closes all the openings. Then the coolies come back and carry her to her destination. Although they cannot be seen, the number of a man's wives is sometimes revealed to the traveller in a peculiar way. In passing through the villages a ceaseless *plunk, plunk, plunk* is heard, which is the sound of the "ironing" of the gentlemen's white clothes by beating them on a smooth stone or piece of wood. The frequency and rhythm of the beats indicate whether one, two, or more wives are engaged in the ironing industry. This, and the preparation of his meals, and the rearing of sons to look after his *post-mortem* interests, are what the men think the women were made for. Love, confidence, and companionship between husbands and wives are almost unknown. Hence there are no homes in Korea. To carry the light of the gospel into these gloomy little prisons and transform them into Christian homes is the work which a trumpet voice of duty and opportunity is now calling the women of our country to do.

Excepting the non-existence of Tauism, Korea is religiously a small *replica* of China. The education of the higher classes is based on the Confucian classics, and the Confucian ethics are their substitute for religion. Confucian ancestor worship prevails among all classes. Buddhism was transplanted from China in the fourth century and soon gained the nominal adherence of the people, but it seems never to have taken very strong hold of the popular mind, and is now far gone in dilapidation and decay. Its temples are few and mean, and its priesthood in such disrepute that, until since the late war, one was not allowed to enter the gates of the capital. Demon worship is universal, but owing to the less serious turn of the Korean mind, it is not quite such a reign of terror as it is in China. Yet it is bad enough, and probably costs the country each year as much as would be necessary to evangelize it from one end to the

Religious.

other. As a defensive apparatus against the demons, we see wooden posts set up on the roads leading into villages, with ugly heads carved at the top, the lips, cheeks, and eyebrows being smeared with red and white paint. Straw ropes, old rags, and wooden figures of birds are hung in the boughs of trees for the same purpose. When, in spite of these obstructions, the demons get into the village, bringing sickness and ill-luck to the people, then the witch doctor comes to the rescue. His equipment consists of various and effective noise-producing instruments, and witch broths, brewed of toads, snakes, lizards, ground-up tigers' teeth, and all the horrible and forbidding things the country affords. These he administers by the bowlful to people with typhoid fever or cholera or small-pox. He also carries a long, sharp needle, which he inserts into whatever part of the victim's body the pain gives evidence of the demon's location, to make a hole to let the demon out! These are successful practitioners to the extent that in a fair proportion of cases they succeed in letting the demon out along with the spirit of the patient.

Such are a few items in the long list of human and Satanic oppressions that afflict this interesting people. May the day soon come when they shall know the truth, and the truth shall make them free.

CHAPTER VIII.

MISSION WORK IN KOREA.

THE history of Protestant mission work in Korea is brief but glorious. Although only fifteen years have elapsed since the work began, a Christian church already exists, containing several thousand members, a church full of life, vigor and aggressiveness, and showing both the disposition and the ability to support and propagate itself.

The first missionaries anticipated much difficulty in carrying on their work from the lethargic character of the people. But the enterprising spirit manifested by those who have become Christians indicates that this lethargy is rather a temporary product of their environment than an innate and ineradicable trait.

Difficulties.

The language is also said to be more difficult of acquisition than either the Chinese or Japanese, with the added difficulty that there are almost no competent native teachers of it available. The native reads the written language with a dreadful and discordant tune, which no foreigner could learn if he would or would learn if he could. Consequently, the process of learning to read is slow and toilsome to the last degree. Learning to talk is even more slow and toilsome, because of the multitude and confusion of honorifics, the misuse of which subjects the speaker to misunderstanding and ridicule. One must indicate to which one of the many social grades the person spoken to belongs by using a different termination to the verb for each grade. The use of "high talk" to a coolie would be as absurd in his estimation as the use of "low talk" to a Yangban would be insulting. Patience and perseverance, however, for about the space of three years, will serve to loose the tongue of any missionary of average linguistic ability, and these difficulties are of small account compared with some that have to be encountered in other fields.

Three things especially combine to make Korea one of the most interesting and hopeful of all mission fields to-day. One is the way the people live, in villages rather than in large cities, rendering them more easy of access and more susceptible of being influenced. Another is the disposition they have shown to help themselves and support their own

Encouraging features.

work. The third is their comparative friendliness to the foreigner. Instead of calling him "foreign devil," like the Chinese, they look up to him with respect and address him as Tai-in —"Great man"—and, although at first somewhat offish and afraid, by a little kindness they are easily won to confidence and friendship. This friendly attitude is perhaps largely due to the fact that from the beginning the medical work has gone hand in hand with, or rather in advance of, the preaching work.

The first resident missionary was Dr. H. N. Allen, of the Northern Presbyterian Board. Soon after his arrival, in 1884, he was called in to sew up some gashes in the person of Mr. Min Yong Ik, a cousin of the Queen, made during a riot at the Palace. In appreciation of this service the king established a hospital, of which Dr. Allen was put in charge. This opened the way for Dr. H. N. Underwood, who came soon after, to begin his evangelistic work. And from that day to this Dr. Allen, Dr. Avison, Dr. Scranton, of the Methodist Episcopal church, and other physicians at Seoül, have, by their ministrations of mercy to the thousands of sufferers who have come to them for help, been constantly making friends for the gospel and securing the government toleration

Medical missions.

MISSION WORK IN THE FAR EAST. 117

ana protection, which have enabled us to carry on our work everywhere, with one or two exceptions, without let or hindrance. Among our pioneer band of Southern Presbyterians is Dr. A. D. Drew, who worked with the other physicians at the capital for the first three years while getting his tongue loosed, and has since been working in the southern provinces where the Southern Presbyterian stations are. He is now known all over the country, and by reason of his work has, I believe, more influence than any other man, native or foreign, in southern Korea. While I was at his home in Kunsan two men came to be treated by him, both of whom had walked from their homes, more than a hundred miles distant. As the result of his unremitting and self-denying labors, and those of other beloved physicians, the way now lies wide open all over southern Korea for our gospel work.

I saw at Seoül a neat church, seating about two hundred people, which the native Presbyte-

Native enterprise. rian Christians there had built entirely by their own exertions and sacrifices. The men wrought with their hands, the women sewed, one man pawned his spectacles, and most of them tithed their incomes of from two to five dollars a month twice over for the cause. In the work of the Northern Presbyterians in the northern provinces thirty-five churches have been built in this way, many self-supporting schools established, and many native workers are spreading the gospel news far and wide, nearly all of them entirely supported by their own people.

The work at our southern stations is in a less advanced stage, but is being conducted on the same self-supporting basis, and is opening up in a way that gives promise of the same kind of success. At Chunju I found Mr. and Mrs. Reynolds, and Mr. and Miss Tate, and Mr. Harrison and Miss Ingold living, not in the palatial residences that certain Oriental travellers on the steamer going over told me the missionaries always lived in, but in the regulation mud huts of the natives, with their little rooms of from six to nine feet square. Here they had been for two years. And yet they seemed as happy as any of the people I know who live in two-story brick houses in this country. At Kunsan I found Dr. Drew and Mr. Junkin with their families and Miss Linnie Davis living not only in the thatched mud huts, but also in the mud when it rained, for they were down in the valley, right among the natives. They were happy also, except that some of them were suffering in health from their surroundings. If all our church at

MISSION WORK IN THE FAR EAST. 119

home could have communicated to it some of their heroic and self-sacrificing spirit, the whole Korean peninsula would soon be resounding with what I heard at the Sunday morning service at Kunsan. About forty men were seated on the floor of the little native dwelling that served for a church. About the same number of women were present. They were required by Korean custom to be invisible, but were permitted to hear and participate in the service through a piece of cheese cloth stretched over the door of an adjoining room. When Mr. Reynolds preached I was impressed by their reverent attention. When he led in prayer they leaned over until their foreheads rested on their hands laid upon the floor. When they sang their words were strange and their voices unmelodious, but I recognized the tune as Coronation, and I knew they were singing in their Korean tongue,

"All hail the power of Jesus' name,
  Let angels prostrate fall;
Bring forth the royal diadem,
  And crown him Lord of all."

Dear reader, we cannot tell what changes the future may bring, but we know that this is the day of the church's opportunity in Korea. God has set before us there an open door, which He will permit no man to shut if we will only enter it. It is in the hope that it may contribute something towards awakening those who read it to the need of the gospel, and to the obligation resting on us to make it known in Japan, China, and Korea that this little volume is sent forth.

APPENDIX.

REPORT TO THE EXECUTIVE COMMITTEE OF FOREIGN MISSIONS, BY THE SECRETARY, ON HIS VISIT TO CHINA, KOREA AND JAPAN, 1897.

To the Executive Committee of Foreign Missions:

I hereby present to you the report of my visit to our missions in China, Korea and Japan. This visit was made in accordance with the advice of the General Assembly sitting at Charlotte, N. C., and with the instruction of the Executive Committee given at its meeting held on June 8, 1897.

The advice of the Assembly was given on condition that the expense of the visit should be provided for without drawing on the Foreign Mission treasury. The committee's instruction was given on receipt of information that a contribution of $100 had been offered from a friend in the city of New York, not connected with our church, and that other contributions, believed to be sufficient, had been offered from other private sources, which could not in any way affect the regular contributions to our treasury. I am glad to report on my return that the expense of the visit was thus fully met.

Leaving home on July 26th, I sailed from San Francisco on August 5th, and reached Shanghai on September 1st. The plan of the visit included an absence of five months, allowing two months for the outward and return voyage, and three months for work in the different fields. Of this time it was arranged to give six weeks to China and three each to Korea and Japan.

In China I visited all the stations of what is known as "The Southern Circuit," except Lingwu, which I was prevented from reaching by continuous rains during my visit to Hangchow. On account of detention by sickness and the impossibility of securing prompt transportation, I was compelled to forego the pleasure and profit of visiting the three northern stations of Tsing-kiang-pu, Suchien, and Chuchow-foo. In Korea I visited Seoul, where the headquarters of the mission are still temporarily located, and the two stations in the southern provinces, Chun-ju and Kunsan, the only ones as yet regularly occupied. In Japan I visited all the stations except Takamatsu,[1] where, at present, we have no resident missionary.

On the ninth day of December I took passage on the Pacific Mail S. S. *China,* reaching San Francisco on December 23d and Nashville on December 28th.

At every point visited, with two or three exceptions, I preached to the native Christians through an interpreter, and also, as opportunity offered, in the street chapels to congregations of unbelievers. Everywhere the native Christians received my visit as an evidence of our special interest in them, and everywhere I was charged by them with messages of love and gratitude to the church at home, and with requests for our prayers in their behalf.

---

[1] Since occupied by the Revs. W. C. and W. McS. Buchanan.

MISSION WORK IN THE FAR EAST. 123

Two weeks of the time given to China were occupied with the exercises of the Thirtieth Anniversary Conference of the Mission, and of the regular annual mission meeting, held at the same time. I also attended the annual meeting of the Korean mission held at Kunsan, and an adjourned meeting of the Japan mission held at Kobe. I participated freely in the deliberations of all these meetings, on the understanding that no advice or opinions I might express concerning matters falling under the jurisdiction of the missions were to be taken as official declarations, or to have any other weight than that to which their wisdom might entitle them. I was thus enabled to gain much valuable information concerning the details of the work. These meetings also furnished the opportunity of becoming personally acquainted with many of the missionaries who were previously known to me only through correspondence, and for establishing bonds of personal affection, which I account as among the most valuable of the results to be attained by my visit to them.

So far from feeling qualified by so brief and hurried a visit, to speak with authority on those questions of method and policy concerning which both missionary societies at home and missionaries on the field have been divided in opinion, I only realize the more how difficult and many sided many of these questions are, and am more than ever convinced of the wisdom of that feature of our revised manual, which devolves on the missions a larger share of responsibility than they formerly had for the management of the work in the field.

In stating certain conclusions to which I was led by my observation of the work, I will speak first of some which concern all of the three missions alike.

Missionary Salaries.

In 1895 the salaries of our missionaries in the East were fixed on the basis of a report made by Rev. J. L. Stuart, in April, 1893, after a visit and careful investigation made by him as to the conditions and cost of living in the three fields, as follows:

	Single Missionaries.	Married Couples.
China,	$500	$ 800
Japan and Korea,	600	1,000

Salaries in Japan have since been reduced, according to estimates sent from that field, to $500 for single missionaries, and $950 for married couples, and in China to $450 for single missionaries, and in Korea $550. These salaries are lower than those of any other missionaries in those fields receiving a fixed salary. (The China Inland Mission, the Christian Alliance, and possibly some others pay a pro rata of the funds received—the salaries being thus contingent as to amount.) Do they now admit of any further reduction consistently with the idea of giving our missionaries "a comfortable and economical support?"

On the one hand, since the date of Mr. Stuart's report, the movement of the rate of exchange has been in favor of the missionaries. The Mexican dollar, then worth about sixty-two and a half cents, is now worth about forty-eight cents, and the Japanese yen, then worth seventy cents, is now worth fifty cents.

On the other hand, the movement of prices, especially in the last two years, has been against them, about in the same degree, except in the interior of China. There the rise in prices has been steady, but less rapid than in Japan and Korea.

For example, Mr. Stuart reported silver prices of leading staples in 1893 as follows: Flour, $9 per barrel; beef, 19 cents per pound; butter, 56 to 60 cents; soft coal, per ton, $4.50 to $6 in Japan, $6.50 to $8.50 in China and Korea.

The prices of these staples at the time of my visit were: Flour, $13 to $16 per barrel; beef, 35 cents to 45 cents per pound; butter, 60 cents to 65 cents in China and Japan, 80 cents to 85 cents in Korea; soft coal, Japan $8 to $10, according to location; China, $10 to $13, according to location; Korea, $17, at Seoul. Prices of other staples have increased about in proportion to these. All the missions are compelled to order a considerable part, and the Korean mission especially a large part of their supplies from San Francisco.

In Korea and some parts of China it is impossible to know whether meat offered for sale in the native markets has been killed or died of disease. In Korea beeves are usually strangled, instead of butchered. Nearly all the children have to be fed on condensed milk, something in the climate seeming to interfere with the ordinary course of nature in that respect. The transport charges on these foreign goods constitute a heavy item of expense, amounting in Korea to from 30 per cent. to 40 per cent. on the original cost. Along with the rise of prices of food supplies there has been, and is now going on, a rise in the price of native labor. Woolen goods are cheap, but cotton goods and other things entering into the make-up of women's outfits are costly. Most of the single women also find it necessary in the interest of their work, to keep house rather than to board. Native ideas of propriety also require them to have a female companion in travelling. For these and other reasons the cost of living is fully as great, if not greater, for single women than for single men.

Dentistry is enormously high, in China the foreign dentists at Shanghai being the only ones accessible. In Japan there are native dentists who work at reasonable rates, but foreign dentists charge about the same as in Shanghai, and to have work done satisfactorily, it is necessary to employ foreign dentists.

On the whole, my conclusion from all I could see and learn in regard to this matter is that the salaries as fixed in 1895, on the basis of Mr. Stuart's report, are as low as they can be made without the danger of subjecting our missionaries to actual hardship and embarrassment. My conviction is most decided that no reduction should be made in the salaries of married missionaries.

Mission Property.

In the matter of mission property our policy has always been to own as little, in foreign lands, as the necessities of the work would allow. I saw nothing that led me to doubt, but much to confirm my belief in the wisdom of this policy.

In China, while the right to purchase land is guaranteed by treaty, the actual purchase is often resisted by the local officials and sometimes becomes the occasion of serious trouble. In Korea we can gain no fee simple title to land except in a treaty port, and in Japan none at all. But in the case of missionary residences, in China the alternative is between the danger of having trouble with, and perhaps temporarily aggravating the hostility of the natives, on the one hand, and the certainty of suffering from climate and environment on the other. In Chinese cities the dwellings, even of the better classes, are packed together on densely crowded streets, and surrounded by indescribable conditions of discomfort and unhealthfulness. The ruling idea in their architecture is the exclusion of sunlight and fresh air. The physical constitution of the Orientals seems, by the power of heredity, to be in some degree adjusted to these conditions. But in the case of Europeans and Americans the battle is always sooner or later a losing one. Several of our missionary families in China are now living in native houses, and in every such case there were one or more members of such families who seemed to me to be suffering in consequence of it. Moreover, in order to preserve the mental and physical condition necessary for their best work, in China especially, our missionaries need homes, to which they may periodically retire, and find rest from the nerve strain produced by the ceaseless pressure of curious, unsympathetic, and hostile crowds.

In Korea, and in the part of the country occupied by our mission especially, it may be said in general that there are no native houses, but only huts, with mud walls and thatched roofs and rooms the size of our dressing rooms and closets. Japanese houses and the conditions surrounding them are better than those of China and Korea, but their walls are all sliding partitions which cannot be made tight enough to afford adequate protection from the winter climate. Leases of ground may be made in Japan for periods of twenty (20) years or more. The rents paid for a native house for ten years will ordinarily be sufficient to build a comfortable foreign style dwelling. My conviction is, therefore, that in all those fields our missionaries should be encouraged to obtain land, with such security of tenure as the case admits of, and build their own dwellings, rather than to risk life or health in attempting to live in native houses.

On the other hand, no matter how much our income may be increased, I trust that no large proportion of it will go into the mission buildings of which I saw so many in the East, planned on a scale which the native church can never hope to rival, producing the impression of unlimited wealth at the disposal of the missions that build them, and thus tending to discourage rather than to stimulate native effort.

Self-Support.

For some years past there has been an effort, more or less united, on the part of the missions and the societies at home to introduce into the work more largely than heretofore, the principle of self-support. I am glad to report that our missions are among the most strenuous supporters of this policy, in all the eastern fields. Our China mission has been noted from the beginning for the economy with which its work in conducted, which fact was more than once mentioned to its praise by members of other missions who took part in our Anniversary Conference. By pursuing a different policy they could have had more visible results of their work to show at the present time; but the foundations they have been laying would have been less solid and enduring; and they can now look forward to a brighter and happier future than if they had sought to force a more rapid development by the lavish use of money.

In Japan, where the opposite policy has been pursued by all the missions, more than elsewhere, the zeal of our mission in the policy of self-support has brought its members in some places into more or less strained relations with leaders of the native church. It is too much to expect of these that they should see the matter from our standpoint, and the problem of changing from the old to the new plan is one that requires to be handled with great tact and delicacy. But in my judgment the change is vital to the future purity and power of the church, and those who are working to that end should receive the earnest sympathy and co-operation of their home societies and boards. With such co-operation, the success of the movement in behalf of self-support in Japan is already assured.

Our Korean work is being conducted from the beginning on the "Nevius Plan" of self-support, and the native Christians there have not learned, and it is to be hoped, will never learn, that there is any other plan.

Medical Work.

I was impressed by all I saw of our medical mission work, with its exceeding value and importance. But so much depends on the work being done in the best way, that only those should be sent as medical missionaries who have had the best training our schools afford, supplemented by some hospital experience. They should also have a full and thorough equipment for surgical work. The amount of $200 allowed by our manual for medical outfit is insufficient for this purpose. It is the judgment of all our medical missionaries with whom I consulted that this amount should be at least doubled. The dispensary work is valuable, but does not furnish the opportunity which is so desirable for spiritual work in connection with the medical work. For this purpose it is necessary that they be furnished with adequate facilities for treating "in patients," which none of them now have except Dr. Wilkinson, at Soochow. It is not the policy of the committee, nor of our missions, to invest Foreign Mission funds in the building of large hospitals. But in order to success of the work, and to securing the best spiritual results from it, the effort should be made to supply each medical missionary, as soon as possible, with means to build some inexpensive rooms where difficult cases can be properly treated and cared for, and where the missionary evangelist can have the opportunity of reaching them.

It was also a common complaint in the hospitals I visited that their evangelistic force was insufficient to follow up the work so as to secure the largest and best results from it. I think that in the future development of our medical work we should look well to this point. The tendency of all "institutional" mission work is to localization, whereas, it seems to me, such work, under the present conditions of the mission problem, is only justifiable when it is so managed that the institution becomes a center of radiation.

CHINA.

Notwithstanding the many and great difficulties that encompass the work in China, in most of the places occupied by our workers, encouraging progress is being made. If I should offer any criticism of our past policy in that field, it would be that there has all along been too much scattering of the forces. Stations have been opened faster than we have been able to man them for effective work, with the results that new missionaries have often been pushed into places of responsibility before they were prepared for it by a mastery of the language, and the work of itinerating the country has suffered.

Most of our centers are in the large cities, where it is necessary, for many reasons, that they should be. But good strategy would seem to require that special emphasis be placed on work in the country, because there is at present the point of least resistance, and because among the farmers in the country villages there is to be found a more hopeful element out of which to gather self-supporting and aggressive churches than that which is mainly accessible to us in the cities. To carry on effective country work from a center in the city, requires at least three men, besides the necessary provision for women's work. There are only three of our China stations having that number of men who have been in the field long enough to do regular work. I would therefore recommend that the committee veto the opening of any more stations in China until all those now occupied have been properly manned.

JAPAN.

The missionary situation in Japan is in some respects critical, and contains many elements requiring wisdom and forbearance in those who have to deal with it. The spirituality of the native church has suffered from the political ferment the country has been in during and since the war with China, and from the influences that have come to it in connection with the opening of foreign trade. Its orthodoxy has suffered from the elimination of the reformed symbols from the creed of the Church of Christ in Japan, and from the importation from this country and from Europe of rationalistic views, especially concerning the word of

God and the doctrine of the atonement. Its activity has been lessened by the too large use of foreign money in the employment of native workers. On the other hand, I had the pleasure of meeting many members of the native church who impressed me as being sound, earnest and praying men, as well as men of character and ability. The establishment of a church of which this can be said, is one of the successes, and not one of the failures of mission work, and its future may be looked forward to with encouragement and hope.

I think it is now generally recognized that, in Japan, mission work in general, and as a consequence, that of the Japanese church which has grown out of it, is subject to the criticism of having been too much confined to one class of the people. When the feudal system was overthrown, the feudal retainers, known as "Samurai," found themselves in the new order of things without a reason of existence. This event, happening just before the country was opened to mission work, furnished the opportunity of reaching this class, which proved readily accessible, and out of it the present membership of the churches has been largely gathered. The present most urgent need is the evangelization of the lower classes. And this is a work which a ministry drawn mainly from the Samurai class, because of the strong class spirit in all Oriental countries, and for many other reasons, cannot reasonably be expected to push with the energy and sympathy necessary to success.

For this purpose an increased number of foreign missionaries is needed, until a native ministry drawn from the lower classes can be raised up. Missionaries for Japan, however, should be selected with greatest care. They should if possible be tried men—men with some degree of maturity, experience, and approved wisdom.   * * *

KOREA.

Apart from some ominous clouds on the political horizon, the whole missionary situation in Korea is cheering in the highest degree. The people are much less anti-foreign than other Orientals. Their friendship is readily won by kind treatment. The Presbyterian missions working in co-operation there are unanimous in support of the self-supporting policy, and consequently there is no difficulty in carrying on the work on that basis. What competent observers have pronounced to be the most interesting and successful mission work now being done in the world is that of the Northern Presbyterians in the province of Pyeng-Yang. The work of our mission in the southern provinces, as yet only two years old, is already yielding results in hopeful conversions and in large numbers of inquirers and adherents. * * * There are few large cities, the people living mostly in villages, rendering them more easy of access, and more susceptible of being influenced. If the field could be at once supplied with a sufficient number of workers, the church might soon have the joy of seeing the whole nation evangelized. *This result can be achieved much more easily before than after the advent of western civilization.* Uneducated Buddhism and Confucianism are much less formidable foes than educated atheism.

Political troubles may also complicate the situation in the future. Now the way is open for almost unhindered gospel work. While in Korea I was continually reminded of the Saviour's words concerning the white fields and the waiting harvest, and I could not help from coveting the privilege offered to those to whom God has given the means that would enable them to say to us, "Find the men who are willing to go and do this work, and we will provide their support."

www.ingramcontent.com/pod-product-compliance
Lightning Source LLC
Chambersburg PA
CBHW030309170426
43202CB00009B/933